RELATIONSHIPS 101

by

James Ranger

Relationships 101
© 2015 by James Ranger
Requests for information should be addressed to:
Ranger Ministries, 4201 Stine Road, Bakersfield, CA 93313

Printed in the United States of America

Relationships 101 / James Ranger [Teresa Haymaker, editor]
ISBN 978-0-9864169-0-3 (pbk.)

DEDICATION

This book is dedicated first to the love of my life, my wife, Lydia, the one with whom I have experienced most of what I've written about in this book. She is my true North Star, my forever-friend.

I also dedicate this work to my sons, Jim and Jonathan, and my god-son, Quellen Andrews. I have had much joy and stress in my father-son relationships through the years and I am so proud of the men they have become.

I also dedicate this book to my daughters-in-laws, Camilla and Amber, and to my god daughter-in-law, Candice. All three of them are very strong and courageous women who have brought so much joy into the life of our family—including the delights of my life, our grandchildren, whom I adore!

I also dedicate this book to my parents, Jim and Margaret Ranger, and my in-laws, Thomas and Pat Patterson. They have had an amazing impact in my life, especially in those formative years.

And the Lord is the one who goes ahead of you;
He will be with you. He will not fail you or forsake you.
Do not fear, or be dismayed.

—Deuteronomy 31:8 NASB

ACKNOWLEDGMENTS

I thank my New Life church family whom I get the privilege of serving as shepherd-leader, for the support and care they have given to my family and me for decades. We've learned, and are still learning, to do life together in life-giving relationships. I love all of them!

I also thank my staff and pastoral team at New Life Center for their partnership with me in changing lives, as we seek to "Bring them in, build them up, train them for, and send them out, all for the glory of Jesus Christ."

I thank Teresa Haymaker for her tireless and patient effort in making this book much better than I could have ever made it by myself. In her editing she has had the hand of a skilled surgeon, cutting only where the right cuts needed to be made.

I thank Wendy Nolasco for her constant "prodding" over the last few years to get this book birthed. Her gentle (and sometimes not-so-gentle) nudges to keep me going and for not giving up on this project is much treasured.

I thank Brett Eastman for his creative heart and mind and for helping me jump-start this book a few years ago.

I thank my lifetime "covenant" friends, Bill and Beth Chaney, for living out these relational principles with me for almost forty years and for their unconditional love, unending support, and consistent friendship.

I thank my mentors who, through the years, have helped shape my thinking about relationships. A few of them are Dr. Wayne Cordeiro, Dr. Rick Warren, Dr. John Maxwell, Bill Hybels, Dr. Pete Kieper, Dr. Harold and Winona Helms.

And most of all, I am eternally grateful to my best friend, the friend who sticks closer than any brother, Jesus Christ, God's Son. Through Him I've learned to truly love and be loved, to love Abba, His Father and my Father, to love others-including my enemies, and to love myself.

Contents

FOREWORD

As I read though the early drafts of this book I realized just how wonderfully strange, unique, and deep the relationship between the author and myself. His accent is weirdly from the north and mine a bit more Texan. We met at church camps as young teens and somehow struck up a friendship. Perhaps because we were both musicians and music became our common language, making our first recording together in 1977.

Over the years, we would see each other at camps and a few meetings here and there. Later, we would both marry and begin families who would grow together as brothers and sisters. My son Derek and daughter Valerie referred to the Rangers as Uncle James and Aunt Lydia. Jim and Jonathan Ranger were like brothers to my kids. We were family. I was asked by James to serve as his associate pastor first in Conway Arkansas, then again in Bakersfield, California. The church was growing and things were rolling. But hard times came: times of rumors of disloyalty and opportunities for division between us caused by certain members of the congregation. Some would pick favorites and try to play one of us against the other with "compliments." Still in our twenties, we all learned hard, discouraging truths about some churched people. But we held on to our covenant relationships. For some divine reason, we all four grasped the concept of covenant relationship and each has proven it and had it proved to them by the others. We walk in a level of friendship most peers and colleagues cannot fathom. It is my pleasure to recommend this book because I know the depths of the heart of the author. I know his discourse to be more than words on paper; rather it flows from a life lived out in transparency and truth.

May God use the words in this book to spark a deeper level of healthy, covenant relationships among us.

Bill Chaney,
Chairman
The Foursquare Church
December 15, 2014

INTRODUCTION

The fact that you've picked up this book on relationships tells me you are looking to improve your already-good relationships, or you're trying to resurrect a bad relationship, or you're on the front-end of life and you're trying to break the relational code so that you can have life-giving relationships the rest of your life. No matter why you picked up *Relationships 101*, I believe it can help you. It can help you because it's based on God's Book about relationships—the Bible; and it's based on my experience in relationships with my family and friends, and as a pastor for 35+ years.

I call this book, *Relationships 101*, because what I write is not anything new or original, but it's foundational to healthy and life-giving relationships. It's what I truly believe are some of the basic essentials.

Now, I waited to write this book until now because I wanted its message to come out of more than theory, book-knowledge, and canned how-to's. I wanted it to flow out of my life-experience as a husband, a father, a friend, and as a pastor-leader.

The ideas I write about here in *Relationships 101* are applicable to every relationship in your life—to your friendships, boyfriend or girlfriend, husband or wife, children, co-workers, etc. With that said, obviously much of my experience in relationships comes from my practice of these ideas with my wife, Lydia, who I've been happily married to for almost 35 years. Yes, we've had our ups and downs since we got married when she was 16 and I was 19. We've had plenty of practice at living out what I've written in this book. So understand that you will read along the way real and raw accounts of how we've worked at our relationship. I share our story throughout this book in the hopes that it will give you hope at working at all your relationships.

Open your heart and mind to what the whispers of the Spirit will be for you as you read *Relationships 101*. Don't just read it, apply it. Allow God to take your relationships to a whole new level as we grow together.

My friend, I am honored that you and I can take this relational journey together. Let's get started!

Your friend, James

Chapter One

COMMUNICATION: AN AMAZING KEY TO GREAT RELATIONSHIPS

The reason we're starting our journey together through this book with this subject of communication is I'm convinced that communication in our relationships will either make them or break them. Whether it's in a marriage, or with your child, or in a friendship, or at work, good communication will allow you to enjoy healthy and fulfilling relationships. On the other hand, nothing can mess up our relationships like miscommunication!

Some time ago I experienced this with one of our sound guys at New Life Center, the wonderful community of faith I serve. During one of our gatherings, the sound guy was doing such an exceptional job of mixing the sound that I leaned over to our service coordinator and said, "Hey, can you please radio the sound guy and tell him the sound is awesome today." She radioed my message to him...so I thought.

After our gathering, I went by the sound booth and told the sound guy, "The sound was great this morning!" He said, "That's not what I heard." I thought he was kidding so I said, "Oh, come on, it really was good." Again, he said, "That's not what I heard."

I asked, "Well, what did you hear?" He responded, "The service coordinator radioed me and said, 'James said to tell you that the sound was *awful*.'" I still thought he was kidding with me so I called the service coordinator over and said, "Please tell Mike what I told you to tell him." She said, "Are you sure you want me to tell him?" I said, "Of course. Go ahead." She said, "Pastor told me to tell you that the sound was awful!"

When I finally stopped laughing, I told him how my message was miscommunicated and went from "awesome" to "awful"! We all laughed and that situation turned out very funny. But what could have happened had I not gone and talked to Mike? What I meant as the highest form of compliment—"You're awesome," would have been received as the highest form of criticism—"You're awful"!

Relationships can go from awesome to awful if our communication is not good.

THE WAY WE COMMUNICATE
AFFECTS EVERY AREA OF OUR LIVES

Does our ability to communicate affect our relationships at work? Sure. Those who can communicate better in the workplace have better working relationships, and they are generally paid better.

Does our ability affect our friendships? You bet. The deeper you can communicate with a friend, the deeper the relationship will be.

How about those of us who are married? Does communication affect us? Absolutely. During a recent survey, 100 divorce lawyers were asked the question, "What is the major cause of divorce in America?" All 100 lawyers agreed that it was lack of communication.

So, how do we improve our communication, and as a result, improve our relationships? One of the major sources of wisdom for learning how to do this is the book of Proverbs, the book of wisdom. Proverbs shows us how to communicate in an "awesome" way at work, at home, and with friends.

First, I would suggest that you **ONLY SAY WHAT NEEDS TO BE SAID**.

Isn't it true that sometimes bad communication comes from us saying too much? Whether it's in your marriage, friendships, or workplace, sometimes we "open mouth and insert foot!" The Bible teaches us to use our words sparingly, and to speak with caution.

Did you know that the Ten Commandments contain 297 words, Psalm 23 has 118 words, the Lord's Prayer is 56 words long, and the Gettysburg Address is 272 words? Yet, in a recent report, the Department of Agriculture needed 15,629 words to discuss the pricing of cabbage. What makes the difference in not the *amount* of words, but the *right* words!

Proverbs says, *"Don't talk too much, for it fosters sin. Be sensible and turn off the flow!"* (10:19 NLT). Have you ever wanted to say that to someone? "Hey, turn off the flow"!

Proverbs also says, *"Those who are careful about what they say protect their lives, but whoever speaks without thinking will be ruined"* (13:3 NCV).

God wants us to be careful about what we say—to get our minds in gear before we engage our mouths, to think before we speak.

A wise old owl lived in an oak
The more he saw the less he spoke
The less he spoke the more he heard.
Why can't we all be like that wise old bird?

To say only what needs to be said I suggest working on a few things. One is—**Don't say everything you know.**

Proverbs says, *"A truly wise person uses few words"* (17:27 NLT).

R. E. Phillips said, "Words are a powerful drug, and many men are destroyed from their much use."

Would you agree with me that there are some things that ought not be said! Have you ever been in the middle of a nice dinner and someone says, "I know we're in the middle of eating and I shouldn't tell you this but…"? And after ruining your dinner you agree, "Yeah, you should not have told me that."

Children are famous for saying things that are better left unsaid. When our son Jonathan was a little boy he had the nasty habit of doing this. For example, there was a time he was in Sunday School class and his teacher said, "Anybody have a song you'd like to sing today?" Jon raised his hand and said, "Let me sing, let me sing." He stood in front of his class and began singing this deeply spiritual song: *"All my Ex's live in Texas."*

After class the teacher came and told Lydia and I what Jon did and asked us where he learned this stuff. Being the honest man I am, I pointed to Lydia! Later, when we got home, I learned the lesson from her that I don't have to tell everything I know.

Many parents wish their kids didn't say everything they know. It's like the little boy who was traveling with his mother. As they approached the airline ticket counter the little guy said, "I am two years old." Suspiciously, the agent looked down at the boy and said, "Young man, do you know what happens to little boys who lie?" The boy smiled and said, "Yep, they get to fly for half price!"

Don't say everything you know. And, also…**Don't say everything you think.**

Proverbs says, *"Even dunces who keep quiet are thought to be wise"* (17:28 MSG). There's a Latin proverb that says, "Keep quiet and people will think you a philosopher."

Have you ever been around a guy who never had a lot to say, and you thought, "Wow, this dude is smart?" But then he opens his mouth and lets the cat out of the bag!

There are a lot of people in our world who "Just speak their mind"; they say whatever they're thinking at that moment. But Proverbs 18:10 says, *"You will have to live with the consequences of everything you say"* (TEV).

If we want to enjoy great relationships then we should not say everything we know or think and, also...**Don't repeat everything you hear**. In other words, don't give in to gossip.

Proverbs says, *"A troublemaker plants seeds of strife; gossip separates the best of friends"* (16:28 NLT). So a gossiper is a troublemaker—they make trouble. If we're known as gossips, who are troublemakers, then that will have a profound effect on our relationships. I mean, do you want to hang out with someone who "tells all to inquiring minds"? No way! You run from folks like that. On the other hand, if you know safe people, who are "secret-keepers" and confidential friends, how quick are you to want to be around them?

As a pastor, the biggest troublemakers I've had to deal with through the years were the gossips. Not the drunks, prostitutes, or drug addicts—the gossips. Why? Because the drunks, prostitutes and drug addicts know they're messed up, but the gossips are in serious denial because they spiritualize it.

For example, Gossiping Gertrude calls up Sister Sally and says, "Oh, I'm so burdened for Jane." Sister Sally asks, "Why are you so burdened?" Gossiping Gertrude says, "Oh, you don't know? Well, let me tell you what's happening so we can pray for Jane." Then for the next hour they have a spiritual gossip session. Later, when they're asked about it, they deny it and say, "Oh, Pastor James, we were just praying about it."

You want to know how I judge if I'm gossiping about someone? It's simple. Gossiping is when we are telling something to someone who is not a part of the problem nor the solution. If they're not a part of the problem nor the solution then what positive results could come from me telling them?

The Bible says that when we're tempted to share others' faults, we have a choice to make, and that choice is found in Proverbs: *"Disregarding another person's faults preserves love; telling about them separates close friends"* (17:9 NLT). The question is, "Do I want to preserve love or destroy it? Do I want to make friends or make enemies? God says it's my choice. I can either disregard peoples' faults or disclose them; I can either give them grace or gossip about them.

If we want to be better communicators, we need to communicate only what needs to be said. And then we need to **only talk when we have all the facts**.

Proverbs says, *"Answering before listening is both stupid and rude"* (18:13 MSG). The NLT translation says, *"What a shame, what folly, to give advice before listening to the facts!"*

At one time or another every one of us have spoken about something or someone before knowing all the facts. Most of the time it happens without any real consequences. But sometimes it can have devastating effects. Remember Richard Jewell? He was the security officer who was first on the scene when the bomb exploded at the 1996 Olympics in Atlanta. He acted courageously—he was truly a hero.

But then the FBI developed suspicions about Jewell, and began to consider him a suspect in the bombing. The FBI was simply doing their job; they needed to suspect everyone. But the media went wild with the story. *The Atlanta Journal-Constitution* printed a story packed with innuendo and misleading comments. *The New York Post* called him a "fat, former failed sheriff's deputy" in a story that crossed the line between reporting him as a possible suspect and declaring him guilty. Even one of the most trusted news commentators compromised his credibility by saying, "They probably have enough to arrest him right now, probably enough to prosecute him. But you always want enough to convict him."

As we all know now Richard Jewell didn't plant the bomb. He really was a hero. He put his life in danger to save other people, and he was ripped to shreds by the press. But this time (for once) the media was held accountable. A number of news organizations, including NBC, settled with Jewell for an undisclosed amount.

The fact is, we can do a lot of damage by speaking before we get the facts, and some of the damage will come back our way. That's why Solomon said, "The talk of fools is a rod for their backs, but the words of the wise keep them out of trouble" (Proverbs 14:3 NLT). Proverbs also says, "A man of knowledge uses words with restraint" (17:27 NIV).

God says, "If you want to be truly happy in life then speak carefully; consider whether or not you have the facts before you speak."

We need to communicate only when we have all the facts; and communicate only what needs to be said; and, then lastly, **communicate only in the most effective ways**.

Proverbs says, "Everyone enjoys a fitting reply; it is wonderful to say the right thing at the right time!" (15:23 NLT). A fitting reply is when we say the right thing at the right time in the right way. So, what is ineffective communication? It's when we give an unfitting reply. It's when we say the wrong thing, at the wrong time, in the wrong way.

How do we communicate in only the most effective way? One way God says we do this is by **NOT QUARRELING**. Proverbs says, "Anyone who loves to quarrel loves sin" (17:19 NLT).

Consider George and Ethel. They had been arguing about everything for years. They didn't know how to communicate effectively and both of them were tired of living in conflict. Ethel says to George, "George, I've been praying for God to help us stop all of this arguing by taking one of us to Heaven. And when He answers my prayer, I'm moving in with my sister."

God wants us to communicate without arguing and quarreling.

As I mentioned in the Introduction, Lydia and I have been married for quite a few years now. Over our journey together we're learning how not to quarrel and argue, but in the early years it was not that way at all. In fact, we were both "professional arguers." We were good at it!

In those early years Lydia and I didn't know how to communicate about our true feelings without having a "debate." And it created some serious pain for us in our relationship. We loved each other deeply, but we didn't know how to communicate effectively.

Finally when we couldn't take it any more we went to a counselor and began to learn how to talk to each other without quarreling. It took a lot of work, time, and patience, but it paid off. And even though we still have relapses from time to time (usually it's me), these days we are doing pretty well at expressing ourselves without quarreling.

What are some of those biblical ideas that helped Lydia and I stop arguing and start communicating? Even though we will cover this subject in more detail in another chapter, let me give you a few ideas on...

HOW TO S.T.O.P. ARGUING
AND START COMMUNICATING

Separate the person from the problem.

Lydia and I used to think they were the same thing. These days we work really hard at expressing love to each other, while honestly dealing with the problem. We have to be able to separate the two—the person and the problem."

Talk about the issue and how it makes you feel.

In the early years, because of my own brokenness, I couldn't stand for Lydia to cry while we discussed problems. And she couldn't stand for me to express anger or frustration of any kind because that made her afraid.

What we've learned is that when she's upset, she cries; when I'm upset, I get angry. Both tears and anger are appropriate, as long as the emotion is controlled and directed at the problem and not the person. Does God cry and get angry? Sure. And so can we—appropriately.

We need to identify the issue and how it makes us feel. We want to say, "Here's the issue, and this is how it makes me feel."

Opt for win/win rather than win/lose.

Do you have any relationships where it's always got to be a win/lose situation? The truth is, nobody wins like that. A lot of husbands find this out; their wife may pretend she's being compliant and allowing the husband to win, but down the road it's going to surface and "it ain't going to be pretty"!

I've seen it happen again and again in marriages where the husband has to have a win/lose in all discussions with his wife. The negative emotions go under the surface...for awhile. And then one day it happens; he comes home from work and finds a little note sitting on the table.

Did he really win all those arguments?

Practice empathic listening and try to understand.

When Lydia and I used to try and resolve conflict it was always me thinking, "I'm going to get her to see it my way if it's the last thing I do." And it usually was! All the time I'd be making my speech Lydia would be sitting there with her arms folded and "her answer running." Neither of us was trying to understand each other.

Then we came across John Gray's book, "Men are from Mars, Women are from (Pluto, I mean) Venus." It helped us learn to truly understand each other. As she says, "James and I have a wonderfully weird relationship...I'm wonderful and he's weird." It's good to know that we understand each other!

Another way of effective communication happens through use of **GENTLE WORDS**. Proverbs says, "A gentle response defuses anger, but a sharp tongue kindles a temper-fire" (15:1 MSG). What defuses anger? "A gentle response." In the Beatitudes Jesus said, "Blessed are the meek (or gentle) for they shall inherit the earth." Why will the meek and gentle inherit the earth? Because they know how to get along with people.

Some husbands reading this are thinking, "Not me, bud. I'm not going to be mousy, meek and mild. I'm a man!" If you think that then you misunderstand meekness. Like the wife who said to her husband, "Are you a man or a mouse? Now squeak up!"

What does it mean to be meek and gentle? Meekness means "power under control." Like a wild stallion that has its energy focused. We can become a gentle-man or a gentle-woman.

What will be the results of gentle communication? Proverbs 15:4 says, *"Gentle words bring life and health"* (NLT). Life and health will come to our relationships.

Another very effective method of communication happens through us using **HEALING WORDS**. Proverbs says, *"Thoughtless words can wound as deeply as any sword, but wisely spoken words can heal"* (12:18 GNT).

What are some healing words we can use to improve our relationships? Here are a few that work almost every time..."I'm sorry," "I was wrong," "I love you," "You matter to me," "Please forgive me."

How many of our families and friendships could be renewed by our simply learning to speak healing words to our kids, spouses and friends? How many of our offices could be renewed by just a few of us employees learning to speak healing words to others?

WITH OUR WORDS WE EITHER BUILD BRIDGES OR BUILD FENCES

Let me tell you about two brothers who lived on adjoining farms.

One day they fell into conflict. It was the first serious rift in 40 years of farming side by side, sharing machinery, and trading labor and goods as needed, without a hitch.

Then the long collaboration fell apart. It began with a small misunderstanding and grew into a major difference. Finally it exploded into an exchange of bitter words followed by weeks of silence.

One morning there was a knock on the older brother John's door. He opened it to find a man with a carpenter's toolbox." I'm looking for a few days work," he said. "Perhaps you would have a few small jobs here I could help you with? Could I help you?"

"Yes," said John. "I do have a job for you. Look across the creek at that farm. That's my neighbor; in fact, it's my younger brother. Last week there was a meadow between us and he took his bulldozer to the river levee and now there is a creek between us. Well, he may have done this to spite me, but I'll go him one better. See that pile of lumber by the barn? I want you to build an eight foot fence so I won't have to see his place or his face anymore."

The carpenter said, "I think I understand the situation. Show me the nails and the post-hole digger and I'll be able to do a job that pleases you."

The older brother had to go to town, so he helped the carpenter get the materials ready and then he was off for the day. The carpenter worked hard all that day measuring, sawing, and nailing.

About sunset when the farmer returned, the carpenter had just finished his job. The farmer's eyes opened wide, his jaw dropped. There was no fence there at all. It was a bridge—a bridge stretching from one side of the creek to the other!

He looked up and saw his younger brother standing by the bridge with his hand outstretched. The brother said, "I can't believe you'd build this bridge after all I've said and done."

The two brothers stood at each end of the bridge, and then they met in the middle and embraced. They turned to see the carpenter hoist his toolbox on his shoulder. "No, wait! Stay a few days. I have a lot of other projects for you," said the older brother.

"I'd love to stay on," the carpenter said, "but I have many more bridges to build."

Friend, with your words you're either building fences or building bridges, you're either healing others or harming others, you're either tearing down or building up.

Always remember the power of your words. *"Words kill, words give life; they're either poison or fruit—you choose"* (Proverbs 18:21 MSG).

I hope you choose words of life that will bring life to all of your relationships.

What kind of communicator will you choose to be?

Chapter Two

CELEBRATE DIFFERENCES

Have you ever prejudged someone by their appearance? Have you ever judged a book by its cover, only to find out down the road that you were dead wrong? I think we all have done that.

The great actor Shrek encountered this. You may remember in the movie, Shrek II, when Shrek and Fiona were summoned to meet Fiona's parents—the King and Queen of Far Far Away. Fiona was supposed to have married the handsome Prince Charming, because he was so handsome. But instead she has married the ogre, Shrek…who has a lot to be desired when it comes to his outward appearance. The king and queen had a hard time looking past Shrek's green skin, funny looking ears, and overgrown head. They didn't take the time to see what was on the inside; a wonderful soul that was very beautiful.

Your biggest problems, and mine, are figuring out how to get along with people who are different than we are.

"To dwell above with those you love, that will be a glory. But to dwell below, with those we know, that's another story."

Whether it's racial differences, or gender differences, or political differences, or religious differences, one of the main keys to getting along with those who are different from us is learning to never judge a book by its cover.

I had to learn this early in my life. Back when I was 8 years old, living in St. Paul Minnesota, my dad was invited to preach at a black church called Robert's Temple, in South Chicago. Remember, this was Chicago in 1968, the same year Dr. Martin Luther King Jr. was assassinated; and we were at this church at the very same time the riots happened at the Democratic Convention. It was a scary time, to say the least.

When we went to this very large black church, with over 1000 folks there for the service, my sisters and I sang for them, and my dad preached. What is forever etched in my heart is the way I felt so loved by people who were so different from me.

I felt very loved, until we walked outside the church. That's when the rocks started flying at our car and the threats on our lives started. I felt love and then hate all in the same experience. Love in the church, and hate outside of it.

Then, when I was 13 years old, my family moved from St. Paul, Minnesota to Columbus, Mississippi. You talk about culture shock! I found out quickly that some of those southern folk, including some Christians, didn't like us Yankees! They prejudged me, thinking I was like those guys who beat them up in the Civil War. I didn't even know anything about the Civil War...but they did! They called me "Yankee" and told me, "The south's gonna do it again."

And then there was the black/white issue in the Deep South. All my life I was raised with African Americans, and some of them were my best friends when I lived up in Minnesota. So I didn't know, at 13, that my daddy had brought us to the heart of KKK country; I didn't know that the schools had just been integrated recently. (I watched riots and fights at my school based solely on the color of skin.) Many times I found myself trying to be the peacemaker. But I often ended up like the guy who didn't want to fight in the Civil War so he wore navy blue pants and a gray shirt...they shot me from both sides.

During that same period of time I got another view of unloving favoritism, but this favoritism wasn't about race, but about religious denominations. Again, this was confusing to me because, as a child, back in Minnesota, I would often go to my dad's Pentecostal church and then go over to my friend's Catholic church, and it was no big deal. But in the Deep South, I discovered the "tribal" differences between the Pentecostals, the Baptists, and the Catholics. To the Pentecostals the Baptists were barely making it to heaven, and the Catholics were definitely not going because the Pope "was the anti-Christ." That's what many preachers back then preached about the Catholic Church.

I didn't know it then, but in that defining, heart-developing time of my life, God was shaping my vision of the kind of Church Family I would one day pastor. He was showing me how I was to live out my life relationally with people who are different from me. God was placing a deep value and a clear vision, inside my soul, of a Church Family where the unconditional love of God would rule all our behaviors and attitudes and relationships.

How can we learn to get along relationally with people who are different from us...whether those differences are gender, religion, personality, or politics? Let me tell you a story about a guy who had to learn how to do this, and we can learn from him. We all know him by the name, Peter. Now, remember as I start Peter's story that up to this point in this newly formed movement, called The Way, only Jewish People were a part of this fellowship. Peter was a devout Jew.

Imagine the scene...Pete is up on the roof at noontime praying. He's getting real hungry, as he smells the good kosher soup brewing down below. About the time he's ready to go downstairs and eat God surprises him with a vision.

Pete goes into a trance and he sees the skies open up and a sheet being let down by all four corners. This is kind of tripping him out, but what he sees next sure enough trips him out. In the sheet he sees all sorts of critters... animals, snakes and birds. And then he hears a voice say to him, "Get up, Peter, kill and eat" (Acts 10:13 NCV). (By the way, that's the scripture deer hunters use to defend their hunting...get up, kill and eat!)

Pete says, "no way, Jose, I'm not going to eat that. It's not Kosher. All my life I've never done that, and I'm not going to start now!" Like all parents have said to their kids, Father God says to Peter, "Pete, eat! If I say something is acceptable, don't say it isn't."

Now, because Pete is so stubborn in changing this lifetime habit, God shows him this same vision three times. Do you relate to that? I certainly do!

Peter comes to himself and is sitting there puzzled by this vision when the Holy Spirit says to him, "There are three men coming to see you, go with them, because I've sent them."

Peter goes downstairs and there are three guys at the front door. They say to Peter, "Our boss, Cornelius, who is a Roman Officer, was visited by an angel who told him to come here and get you, and that you were to come to his house."

Pete and these three guys jump into their camelac and head on down to Caesarea. When they get there to Cornelius' house the first thing Pete says is, "*You know it is against our laws for a Jewish man to enter a Gentile home like this or to associate with you. (Can't you hear his discomfort, being in a non-Jewish home for the very first time in his life?) But God has shown me that I should no longer think of anyone as impure or unclean*" (Acts 10:28 NLT). Peter replied, "*I see very clearly that God shows no favoritism. In every nation he accepts those who fear him and do what is right*" (Acts 10:34-35 NLT).

Right after this Peter tells Cornelius and his family about the true Messiah, Jesus of Nazareth. And as he's telling them about Jesus, suddenly the Holy Spirit fell on all of them and they began to worship God in languages that they had never heard before.

The Jewish brothers, who had come with Peter, kind of freak out, "What is this? The Holy Spirit that was given to just us Jewish believers has now been given to these non-Jewish believers? How can this be?"

Pete says, "Well, the next step is for these new believers to be baptized in water." Little did Peter or Cornelius realize how epic this event would be in history. Because now, The Way had moved from being exclusively Jewish, to including all non-Jewish People as well.

This was great, but it was also challenging, because anytime you meld together people who are different from each other you're going to have challenges. How do you learn to get along with people who are different from you? How do we move from tolerating each other to truly enjoying each other...not in spite of the differences, but because of the differences?

From this awesome story of Peter's breakthrough into connecting with those who were different than him, let me give you a few guidelines on how we, too, can overcome our differences, our prejudices, and our tendencies to show favoritism toward people who are "like our kind."

HOW DO WE OVERCOME PREJUDICE IN OUR LIVES?

First, **allow god to reveal any prejudice or favoritism in my heart.**

In order for this change to happen in Peter he had to be open to God showing him that he had been stereotyping all non-Jewish people. He had been thinking throughout his life, "All non-Jews are unclean, so I can't hang with them."

Nowadays, stereotypes that might cause us to prejudge others, might include:

"All teenagers are rebellious"
"All men are pigs"
"All women are temperamental"
"All white men can't jump"
"All white (or African American, Latino, or Asian) people are like that"

What is favoritism? It's when we favor one type of person over another. Peter found out in a major way that God doesn't do that. He found out that God loves the non-Jew as much as he loves the Jew.

This is one area in which I am so proud of the Church Family I get to serve as pastor, New Life Center. Over the last few decades we've worked really hard to overcome favoritism. Let me share a little of our journey.

We've worked really hard to overcome **RACIAL FAVORITISM**.

When Lydia and I first came to our church family to be the lead pastors, we were 99.99% Anglo. And I stood up and said, "By God's grace, someday we're going to be a Church Family made up of people from every ethnicity in San Joaquin Valley." That was a statement of faith, a dream. And after a few decades we are living out that dream! If you were to show up at one of our weekend gatherings you would see thousands of people representing all ethnicities, nationalities, and diversities.

We've also worked hard to overcome **ECONOMIC FAVORITISM**.

We realize that poor folk AND rich folk need Jesus Christ! And we are here for both! It's possible to be biased toward either group.

We've also worked hard to overcome **GENDER FAVORITISM**.

In many communities of faith they say, "Yeah, you women can bake cookies, have our kids, and teach our little kids, but you can't play any major leadership role in our church." Years ago, at New Life, we made a decision (based on the scriptures as we see them) that both men and women ought to share their gifts of leadership in our church family. We have great male pastors and we have great female pastors. We involve both males and females in every tier of leadership.

We've also worked hard to overcome **GENERATIONAL FAVORITISM**.

We decided that our church family would not be just for the old, or the young; we are for all generations. We are multigenerational. The so-called "experts" say this can't be done, but every weekend we see some families that have five generations coming to church together at one time! Isn't that the way it's supposed to be?

If we are to overcome prejudice and favoritism we must first ask God to reveal to us whether we have it in our hearts...and then ask Him to help us start to deal honestly with it.

Another thing we can do is make the effort to connect with someone different. Now, let's be honest; it would be much more comfortable for seniors to just hang with seniors, and young folks to just hang with young folks. Right? Sure. Why? Because it takes little effort to connect with someone who's just like you, who likes your kind of music, your kind of food, your kind of stories, and your kind of habits. But it takes a lot of effort to connect with someone who is very different from you.

For example, it takes a lot of effort for:
A cowboy to connect with a city slicker
A tatted up dude to connect with one of those sweet little old ladies
A white-collar worker to connect with a blue-collar worker
A Dallas Cowboys fan to connect with a 49's fan
A Protestant to connect with a Catholic
A Democrat to connect with a Republican

It takes a lot of effort. That's why the Bible says: *"Try your best to let God's Spirit keep your hearts united. Do this by living at peace"* (Ephesians 4:3 CEV).

Think about Peter. Did this devout Jew have to make some serious effort to connect with this Gentile, Cornelius? You bet. It took emotional energy. Don't you think he was uncertain about what lay in front of him when he went to this Gentile's home? Maybe he was nervous about doing something he had never done before in his life. Or, maybe he was concerned with what folks might say. (He seemed to always have a problem with that!)

It also took physical energy. The Bible says, *"The next day Peter started out with them, and some of the brothers from Joppa went along. The following day he arrived in Caesarea"* (Acts 10:23-24 NIV).

Peter had to travel from Joppa to Caesarea. How far is that? It's about 30 miles and was done walking or on the back of an animal. This wasn't an easy trip.

I think it's interesting that God required Peter do this. First, because Peter was a day or two journey away, while another church leader, by the name of Phillip, was stationed right there where Cornelius was. Why in the world did God want Pete to experience this? Maybe he had some serious stuff in his heart that had to be confronted. But, secondly, God made Peter come to Cornelius instead of having Cornelius come to him. Why? By doing that, maybe God was saying to all of us, "If you're going to overcome your prejudices and your differences, you can't wait for the other person to come to you, you have to take the initiative and go to them."

Peter also had to be willing to be criticized, because he was. He was criticized for eating with non-Jews. You say what's the big deal? Well, to an orthodox Jew, table-fellowship was, and is, very important. If I'm Jewish and I eat a meal with you it means I accept you. It means we are friends.

Notice what happened to Peter. *"So when Peter went up to Jerusalem, the circumcised believers criticized him and said, 'You went into the house of uncircumcised men and ate with them'"* (Acts 11:2 NIV).

The truth is, if you make the effort to "reach across the aisle," so to speak, then you're going to be criticized.

Over the years, when I've tried to reach out to my Catholic friends, some of my Protestant friends said, "What are you doing? Don't you know they're Catholic?" (Like they've got cooties or some disease.)

When I've tried to reach out to the gay person who comes to our Community of Faith, I've had church folks says, "Pastor James, you're compromising. You need to condemn them, not reach out to them." (As if the homosexual doesn't need God's truth and grace.) The reason why our Church Family has seen so many gay people come out of that lifestyle into freedom, and start living God's ideal for healthy sexuality, is because we've loved them where they were, until God brought them to where He wanted them to be. You can accept someone without approving of their behavior!

When we try to reach out to those who are ethnically different from us and connect with them, there is always a cost. When we try to reach out to our spouse, or to someone of the opposite sex, and connect with them, there is always a cost.

The fact is, it always cost us time, energy, and even criticism when we reach out to those who are different from us.

I also want you to see one more thing in Peter's situation. Pete took the time and energy to "break bread" with someone different from himself. Let me ask you a personal question: "When was the last time you broke bread—had table-fellowship in your home—with someone totally unlike yourself, someone with whom it took a lot of effort to connect?

That's what Jesus would do. And that leads us to the next step of overcoming our biases. **We must desire to be more like Jesus Christ.**

2000 years ago, Jesus caused quite a scandal because He loved to have "dinners with sinners." He regularly had table-fellowship with beggars, prostitutes, tax collectors, social outcasts and those who seemed religiously inferior. And just like with Peter, the religious leaders were outraged at Jesus, because they felt these "dinners with sinners" gave God a bad name.

Remember, in Luke 19, when Jesus said to Zacchaeus, that midget-sized, corrupt IRS agent, "Hey, I'm going to your house today and we're having dinner together?" Why was Jesus inviting Himself to have dinner with a sinner? Because He was looking beyond the outward appearance of this short, arrogant, rip-off artist and He was seeing a heart that was hungry for God. He didn't pre-judge Zacchaeus.

By eating with Zacchaeus, Jesus was offering him a fresh beginning, new dignity, and a friendship with God. Isn't that the Jesus we want to imitate? We don't want to imitate the Jesus of the Crusaders, of the Middle Ages, who slaughtered thousands of people, under the banner of the cross, just because they were of a different religion. We don't want to imitate the Jesus of the KKK who, in the name of Jesus, spewed out hatred, prejudice and bigotry.

We want to imitate the Jesus of the Bible who has dinners with sinners and eats with those who are different from Him. We want to imitate the Jesus of the Bible who accepts and welcomes all people—no matter their country, culture, creed, or color.

Another way we overcome our prejudice is to always be aware of this lurking enemy. Just because I've dealt with prejudice or favoritism in the past doesn't mean I can let my guard down. As long as we live we'll have to deal with this enemy.

In our story, Peter confronted his prejudice, but then decades later, that enemy reared its ugly head again in a major way in Peter's life. Some demons die hard!

The Bible says, *"But when Peter came to Antioch, I had to oppose him to his face, for what he did was very wrong. When he first arrived, he ate with the Gentile Christians, who were not circumcised. But afterward, when some friends of James came, Peter wouldn't eat with the Gentiles anymore. He was afraid of criticism from these people who insisted on the necessity of circumcision. As a result, other Jewish Christians followed Peter's hypocrisy, and even Barnabas was led astray by their hypocrisy"* (Galatians 2:11-13 NLT).

We must always be aware of this lurking enemy, so that we can defeat him.

God gives us another powerful way to overcome our prejudices, and that is, Celebrate Our Differences. First, celebrate how you are different from others. Did Peter lose his Jewish, cultural ways because he connected with this non-Jew? No. Did Cornelius lose his Gentile, cultural ways because he connected with this Jew? No. They still enjoyed their own uniqueness.

Now, later down the road a bunch of zealots tried to force the non-Jews to take on the Jewish customs, but God told them, "Knock it off; don't do that.

You be your Jewish self, and enjoy being yourself, but don't try to force your customs and preferences onto them."

If God had you born into this world as a certain race, or gender, or wonderfully-weird-personality, then celebrate your race, or gender, or wonderfully-weird-personality, while at the same time celebrating the same thing in everyone else.

Celebrate your differences! But then, celebrate the differences of others. Don't criticize them, celebrate them! The Bible says, *"My brothers, as believers in our glorious Lord Jesus Christ, don't show favoritism"* (James 2:1 NIV). Don't think that one person is better than another, celebrate their differences!

A few years ago I wrote a song with that title; *Celebrate Differences*. I wrote that song out of an experience that I had. Let me tell you the story.

A good friend of mine, Jose Arredondo, invited me to play in a golf tournament at the Country Club. This man was Latino and a very successful businessman in our community.

While at this tournament, Jose was walking out in front of me talking to someone else, and two men were right behind me who didn't know that I was his guest. They began saying things about my friend that were racist and very unkind. And frankly, stupid!

I turned and looked at them, and for a moment I almost lost my religion, but I was Jose's guest, and they were way bigger than I was. (A guy's got to know his limits!)

I was very angry at their unkindness and their mean comments that were based solely on the color of this man's skin. I went directly home after this golf tournament and sat down and wrote these words to this song.

CELEBRATE DIFFERENCES

"Why judge my brother by the color of his skin,
Never taking the time to look deep within.
To look at his heart and see what God sees,
A rare and unique person, a whole lot like me!"

"Celebrate differences; let's not criticize.
Let's love like God loves, with colorblind eyes.
Celebrate differences; then we'll realize,
We are bound by God's family ties."

"For God so loved the world, that He gave His only Son.
Not just for a few, but for everyone.
The black and the white, brown, yellow and red.
We are all so special; He died in our stead!"

"Around the throne of heaven I see a crowd
Gathered from all nations, they sing out loud!
No more prejudices in that land, united by our Savior
We walk hand in hand!"

Isn't that a picture of the Kingdom that is to come? Someday in heaven it will be that way. But until then Jesus taught us to pray daily, "Thy Kingdom come Thy will be done on earth as it is in heaven." What are we to pray and strive for on earth, that's in heaven? In heaven there are racial differences and they are celebrated! The Bible says they are there in Paradise from all nations, tribes, and languages. We are to pray for that right now.

In heaven there are no religious denominations. Only true worshippers, focused on Jesus Christ, are there. We are to pray for that now, for unity among believers whose only focus is our love for Jesus. In heaven there are no rich or poor divisions. In fact, everyone is rich! The Bible says that God paves His streets with gold! While we are on earth we are to pray for and assist the poor, and not make class distinctions.

The truth is we are all equal in God's eyes! Jesus, at the cross, changed everything! In Christ we all have freedom and oneness! The Bible says, *"For now we are all children of God through faith in Jesus Christ, and we who have been baptized into union with Christ are enveloped by him. We are no longer Jews or Greeks or slaves or free men or even merely men or women, but we are all the same—we are Christians; we are one in Christ Jesus"* (Galatians 3:26-28 TLB).

The Good News of Jesus is the Good News of freedom. Like Dr. Martin Luther King Jr. said, in possibly the most impacting speech in the last one hundred years, "I have a dream that one day this nation will rise up and live out the true meaning of its creed: 'We hold these truths to be self-evident: that all men are created equal...' I have a dream that my four children will one day live in a nation where they will not be judged by the color of their skin but by the content of their character.... When we let freedom ring, when we let it ring from every village and every hamlet, from every state and every city, we will be able to speed up that day when all of God's children, black men and white men, Jews and Gentiles, Protestants and Catholics, will be able to join hands and sing in the words of the old Negro spiritual, 'Free at last! Free at last! Thank God Almighty, we are free at last!'"[1]

Friend, there is no greater sign of Christ's love, than when two totally different people can sit together and worship together and eat together and do life together. They may have nothing in this entire world in common, but they have Christ, and Christ has always been the great unifier.

Peter and Cornelius were from two different worlds. Peter a Jew; a salty old sea-dog, a fisherman. Cornelius, a non-Jew; a refined, noble, Roman officer. They had nothing in common, except Christ. But when we have Christ, and His cross, that's all that matters. Because of the cross of Christ we are all one. The ground is level at the foot of the cross.

Why don't you celebrate differences today?

---

1   Martin Luther King, Jr., "I Have a Dream," speech, August 28, 1963.

*For now we are all children
of God through faith in Jesus
Christ, and we who have been
baptized into union with Christ
are enveloped by him. We
are no longer Jews or Greeks
or slaves or free men or even
merely men or women, but
we are all the same—we are
Christians; we are
one in Christ Jesus.*

Galatians 3:26-28 TLB

Chapter Three

OVERCOMING BITTERNESS

One of the most important keys to fantastic relationships and emotional health is **overcoming bitterness**. Medical doctors and psychologists agree with what the Bible says about bitterness, that it is one of the most destructive emotions we will ever deal with, and nothing so impacts our relationships as bitterness.

What is bitterness? We use the word bitter to describe something that has a sharp or unpleasant taste, or is hard to bear, such as "a bitter defeat" or a "bitter failure." We also use bitter to describe something that causes us to feel grief, like the death of a loved one—it's a "bitter loss." Or something that causes pain—like "bitter remarks" or the actions of a "bitter enemy." Or, we say "That guy fought to the bitter end."

This subject hits pretty close to home for me because a few years ago I was shocked to find out, from God, that I had some serious bitterness in my heart. It happened on August 29th, 2005 in the early morning. I was in my quiet time reading Psalm 73, minding my own business, when suddenly the Holy Spirit lovingly, yet bluntly, showed me that I had allowed bitterness into my heart, and it was impacting my relationships.

Honestly, it was one of the biggest shocks of my life, because I would never have guessed it. I tend to be an upbeat, positive person, who, when I am wronged and can't seem to get over it, I will go to that person quickly and try to resolve the offense.

That morning, on August 29th, began a journey of inner healing for me that has since greatly improved my inner life and my relationships. From Psalm 73 let me share with you what I learned that day about the CAUSES of, and CONSEQUENCES of, and CURES for bitterness.

WHAT ARE THE CAUSES OF BITTERNESS?

The first cause is when an injustice has been done to me.

Psalm 73 is written by a worship leader named Asaph. Asaph is a lover of God, he goes to church, he lives a morally decent life, but, he has allowed his heart to get bitter over what he feels to be an injustice. Here are his words:

> "Truly God is good to Israel, to those whose hearts are pure. But as for me, I came so close to the edge of the cliff! My feet were slipping, and I was almost gone. For I envied the proud when I saw them prosper despite their wickedness. They seem to live such a painless life; their bodies are so healthy and strong. They aren't troubled like other people or plagued with problems like everyone else. They wear pride like a jeweled necklace, and their clothing is woven of cruelty. These fat cats have everything their hearts could ever wish for! They scoff and speak only evil; in their pride they seek to crush others. They boast against the very heavens, and their words strut throughout the earth. And so the people are dismayed and confused, drinking in all their words. 'Does God realize what is going on?' they ask. 'Is the Most High even aware of what is happening?' [In our darkest moments I think we all have felt like that—"Is God even aware of what is happening in my life?"]
>
> Look at these arrogant people—enjoying a life of ease while their riches multiply. Was it for nothing that I kept my heart pure and kept myself from doing wrong? All I get is trouble all day long; every morning brings me pain." (Psalm 73:1-14 NLT)

What is Asaph saying? He's saying, "It's just not fair! I live a good, moral life and yet I'm not prospering like those who are blatantly immoral. God, why do bad things happen to good people and good things happen to bad people?"

Asaph reminds me of my son Jonathan when he was two or three years old. When things didn't go his way he would scowl and pooch out his bottom lip and say, "It's just not fair!" To this day Jonathan has a strong sense of fairness.

The fact is, there are those of us who are more concerned with fairness and justice then other folk, and therefore we are more bent toward bitterness then others. But we're in good company, because when I looked at all the stories in the Bible of people who became bitter I found that they all felt the same way..."It's just not fair." They had a strong sense of fairness.

When Job lost all of his health, wealth and family, except for his nagging wife, he bitterly complained to God, "It's just not fair" (he may have been thinking, "God, You should have taken her too."). When Naomi lost her husband and her two adult sons to untimely death, she bitterly said, "It's just not fair." When Jacob stole the birthright from his brother Esau, Esau cried bitter tears, "It's just not fair." When the Jewish people became slaves to the Egyptians they cried out with bitter tears, "It's just not fair." When life seems to be unfair and unjust to us we can become bitter.

Another cause of bitterness is when I suffer loss (verse 14).

Someone once said, "Bitterness is loss frozen in resentment." Bitterness grows out of our refusal to let go when someone or something is taken from us. It happens when we suffer the loss of a loved one, or a job, or a relationship.

Asaph got bitter because he felt he was losing out on some money. Did you know that all the people in the Bible that got bitter, got bitter over money or possessions? Job did. Naomi did. Esau did.

Have you ever known somebody to lose their wealth and get bitter over it? I saw this happen after 9/11, and after the stock market crash of 08', when the market hit bottom and many people lost their shirts. Because it was an injustice and a loss, some people couldn't get over it and it turned into bitterness. It's so easy to do!

Any time we lose someone or something dear to us it causes grief. And grief takes time to work through. In fact, many psychologists believe that there are 7 stages of grief we go through when we lose something or someone:

1. Denial. "This can't be happening to me!"
2. Shock.
3. Guilt. "I must have done something wrong."
4. Depression, "Life is now meaningless!"
5. Anger. "How dare anybody come and change my world? It's not fair!"
6. Bargaining. "If only I hadn't said that, or If only I had said that; or if only I could go back and do it over!"
7. Letting go. We accept it and we move on.

Bitterness happens when we get stuck in the stages of anger and bargaining, and we don't move on to letting go.

Another cause of bitterness is when someone prospers who I consider "less deserving" than me (verses 12, 13).

Asaph says, "Who are they to get ahead? Why not me? I'm better than them." Have you ever felt like that? This happens when someone at work gets promoted ahead of you and you feel, "Man, they're a dweeb. I'm smarter, more loyal and better looking than them." It happens when someone else wins the beauty contest instead of you, and you feel, "I should have won. She's not as pretty as I am. Well, I guess, with all that plastic surgery, how could she not win?"

No matter the causes of bitterness, there are always **CONSEQUENCES of bitterness.** What are they?

One of the consequences of bitterness is, it *causes anger*. *"In your anger do not sin...Get rid of all bitterness, rage and anger, brawling* *and slander, along with every form of malice"* (Ephesians 4:26, 31 NIV). Notice how anger and bitterness are twins.

This says to "Get rid of bitterness, rage...malice." What's malice? It's when rage and bitterness produce, "A desire to harm others or to see others suffer; to spite them."

Malice is what happens when the woman who won the beauty contest instead of you is walking down the runway, and as you're applauding with the crowd, behind your plastic smile, you're thinking, "I hope she trips and falls flat on her face. I hope she has something between her teeth when she smiles. Man, I'd like to crown her, all right. I'd like to push that crown clean down into her scalp!"

That's the wrong kind of anger. But there is a right kind of anger. As we will be saying throughout this book, anger is not a bad emotion. There are many losses, injustices, and hurts that we should be angry about. The key is "in your anger do not sin." We sin when we get stuck in our anger and it turns sour in our souls, and we become bitter.

Another consequence of our bitterness is it *creates roots*. The Bible compares bitterness to a tap root that grows up into a large plant. *"Work at living in peace with everyone...Look after each other so that none of you fails to receive the grace of God. Watch out that no poisonous root of bitterness grows up to trouble you, corrupting many"* (Hebrews 12:14-15 NLT).

Do you know what the problem is with letting the bitter root stay there rather than digging it out? The longer you let it grow the harder it is to get out. That's why we must get rid of the root of bitterness as soon as we realize we've got it.

The Bible says that "many are corrupted by its poison." Have you ever been having a great day with a great attitude, but then you got around a critical, grouchy, cynical person? What happens? Before you know it you get infected by their poisonous, bitter spirit.

Bitterness causes anger, creates roots and it also *Corrupts Conversation*. Sometimes we get bitter over something and then we say something we later regret. Moses did this. The Bible says, *"They made Moses angry, (embittered his spirit) and he spoke foolishly"* (Psalm 106:32 NLT).

How many friendships and family and business relationships have been damaged because someone got bitter in the relationship and they ended up blurting out things they later regretted?

Now, those are the causes and consequences of bitterness. But what are the...**CURES for bitterness?** What did Asaph do that we can do (Psalm 73:21-28)?

The first thing I can do is to *face the truth about my bitterness.* Tell God, "God, this is a bummer, I don't like it. My heart has become hurt and bitter. Can you please help me with it?"

That's what Asaph did, he came face to face with his bitter heart. He said, *"THEN I REALIZED how bitter I had become, how pained I had been by all I had seen"* (verse 21).

I remember when, on August 29th, 2005, I had my *ah ha* moment, when I realized how bitter I had become over some hurts. I faced it and confessed it to God and to some friends. And that started major emotional healing in my heart, and as a result it started to improve my relationships as well.

The next thing I can do to cure bitterness is to *free myself by trusting God.* To free ourselves from resentment, bitterness and unforgiveness we have to put our trust in God. To get our hearts soft and tender again we must choose to trust again in God's character, God's promises, and God's ability to make things right. We have to get the big picture again, to see things from God's perspective.

This is what Asaph did, and it was freeing! How did he do this? How can you and I do this? Here are a few things we can do:

• Confess my own foolish heart....(vs 22)

- Remember my belovedness to Abba...(vs 23)

- Remember my ultimate "glorious destiny" is not this life, but REAL life to come. Compare my glorious destiny with the destiny of the wicked. (vs 24)

- Remember that having God in my life is everything, and God should be my main desire—not stuff, not prosperity, not jobs, money, cars and homes. (vs 25)

- Accept the fact that life has its troubles and this is not heaven. (vs 26)

- Know that even when bad things happen to good people God is the strength of their heart. (vs 26)

- Rest my heart in the knowledge that, 1) God is always near, and 2) God is always sovereign and in control. (vs 28)

Asaph said, "*But as for me, how good it is to be near God!* **I have made the Sovereign LORD my shelter**, *and I will tell everyone about the wonderful things you do*" (Psalm 73:28 NLT).

He said, "**I have made...**" That's a choice. You and I can choose to trust the sovereignty of God. "*I have made* **the Sovereign LORD...**" I must recognize that God is God, always in full control, and He alone calls the shots in this life and in the life to come. "*I have made the Sovereign LORD* **my shelter**." When I know that the Sovereign LORD is in my life watching over me, then I can find rest in that. I'm sheltered safe in the arms of God.

Friend, when we trust in Him to take care of all the situations in our lives that seem unfair or unjust, we experience real freedom in our hearts.

Another cure for bitterness is to forgive others. This issue of forgiveness is sprinkled throughout this book because it really is one of the primary keys to great relationships. And it is certainly a key to beating bitterness.

"*Get rid of all bitterness...be kind and compassionate to one another,* **forgiving each other, just as in Christ God forgave you**" (Ephesians 4:31, 32 NIV). How many marriages, or friendships, or relationships at work or in our community of faith are better instead of bitter because we chose to forgive? Forgiveness is powerful!

In 1988, when Lydia and I first came to New Life Center, the community of faith I've been privileged to serve, the church had suffered a very painful church split just before we came. About two-thirds of the church had left with the pastor, and only a small core group of about 45 remained.

Those who remained were broken, wounded, and somewhat bitter toward those who had left, because of the hateful and spiteful way they left. And because of their pain, for the first six months after coming to be their pastor, God had me speak constantly on love, acceptance and forgiveness.

The interesting part of this story is one year before this, these same people I was now pastoring had chosen not to vote Lydia and I in as their pastors. And as a result my heart had been sick and hurt over it and I had to work through my own unforgiveness and bitterness. And God, in His sense of humor, brings me back to the very same people who had hurt me, and now I was helping them work through their unforgiveness, pain, and bitterness.

Over those six months of walking them through love and acceptance, God began to slowly but surely bring healing to many of them.

And then the day came when there was the test of their healing from their bitterness. After those first six months I got a call from one of people who had left New Life and gone with the group who had left. They were crying and asked me and New Life to forgive them. I said, "Of course we will."

And then they asked me if about forty of them could come back. Before I thought I said, "Of course, you can." They hung up and I hung up, and then a thought hit me, "What have I just done? Those people who left here, mean and belligerent, are coming back, and I haven't even asked the New Lifers if it was okay. Those people are going to walk in the church and we just might have World War III."

As that Sunday morning approached for the wayward bunch to come back I was praying! Was I ever praying! The day came and all of the core group who had stayed showed up for church. And then the back doors of that little church opened up and the group that had left walked in. (By the way, I stayed up on the stage away from the action...just in case I needed to "pray" some more!)

My fears were quickly melted as I saw one of the most beautiful scenes I had ever seen. I saw God's love in action. Those people who had done so much wrong and hurt to our core group were very sheepish and reserved as they walked in. But then our group walked up to them and started hugging them and saying, "Welcome back. We missed you. We love you." Tears were being shed; people kept holding onto each other saying, "Please forgive me. I'm so sorry."

I stood there on that stage and wept with them as I saw the unconditional love, acceptance and forgiveness I had been teaching about come into action.

Those original forty-five members that we began with overcame their bitterness by allowing God's love to heal them, and flow through them.

I am convinced that event set the course for the effectiveness we've enjoyed over the last quarter of a century as a church family of restoration, bringing healing to hurting people. Abba Father smiled on all those people's forgiveness way back then and has blessed thousands of others since because of it.

Now, what happens if we don't forgive? We will become "a bitter old man" or "a bitter old woman." Have you ever noticed that we never say, "A bitter young man" or "bitter young woman"? Why? Because early in life hurts and offenses haven't stockpiled yet. But as we age, lots of bad stuff happens along the way, and if we don't process the pain right it turns into bitterness and we become a bitter old man or a bitter old woman.

On the other hand, do you want to stay young in spirit until you die? Learn to forgive daily, and then you will keep your spirit youthful.

Part of forgiveness includes this next step, *forfeit the right to my justice system*. When you and I get hurt don't we take jurisdiction and have our own little Law and Order? Don't we all have our own internal justice system where we demand fair payment? Sure we do!

What is our justice system like?

- I'm the **detective**—I get the facts.
- Then I turn the case over to the **prosecuting attorney**—me—and I make my case of how wrong they are.
- Then I turn the case over to the **judge and jury**—me—and I make sure they're found guilty.
- Then I turn the case over to the **executioner**—me—and I carry out the punishment.

I heard about a person who took justice into her own hands, her name is Lady Sarah Graham Moon. In 1992, at the age of 55 she was dumped by her British aristocratic husband, and she became a "bitter old woman." She decided to implement her justice system with her unfaithful spouse. To begin with, she poured gallons of paint on his cherished BMW while it was parked in his girlfriend's driveway. A week later she cut four inches off the left sleeve on thirty-two of his custom made, $1600, Saville Row suits. And then the following week she gave away sixty bottles of his finest wine.

This lady became somewhat of a celebrity because of the press she received and people began to write to her. One lady wrote and told how she took justice into her own hands by cleaning the toilet with her unfaithful husband's toothbrush, and then watched with delight as he brushed his teeth.

"Dear friends, never avenge yourselves. Leave that to God, for he has said that he will repay those who deserve it" (Romans 12:19 TLB). This means that I forfeit my right to my justice system and give up all jurisdiction to God.

You say, "James, why should I do that?" Because God will do a lot better job than you. He's got ways and means you can't even dream of.

There is one last step to curing bitterness, and that's to focus on keeping my spirit unpolluted. The Bible says, "Watch out that no poisonous root of bitterness grows up to trouble you" (Hebrews 12:15 NLT). God says, "Watch out, James, be on your guard; keep a look out for bitterness in you. You are not responsible for anyone else's spirit. But you are responsible for you. Only you can keep a bitter root from taking hold in you."

What is the key to getting rid of bitterness and keeping a sweet spirit? This key is found in the story of the Jewish people who had just left Egyptian slavery and were traveling across the hot desert when they ran out of water. They were so thirsty, and then suddenly came up on an oasis that had water. They anxiously started drinking it and immediately spit it out—the water was bitter. They actually called this place, "Marah," which means bitter water.

They complained to Pastor Moses and he talked to God about it. God showed him a tree and said, "Moses, cut down the tree and throw it in the bitter water and the waters will become sweet." Moses cut down the tree, threw it in the water, and miraculously the bitter became sweet. And the people drank their fill and their thirst was satisfied.

If the truth were known, some of you reading this have walked across the hot desert of life, and you've drank of the bitter waters of disappointments, hurts, and injustices. God brought you to this moment to show you a tree. The tree is The Cross, the Cross on which Jesus Christ died to make your bitter waters sweet.

Why don't you open your heart to the healing power of the cross?

As I bring this chapter to a close I want to share with you the prayer I wrote in my devotions on August 29th, 2005, when God began to heal the bitterness in my heart. And as I do maybe you will want to pray something like it to God as well.

> "Sovereign LORD, Jehovah God who is always in control, I come to you as humbly as I know how, a broken man who has been arrogant and proud. I have become so bitter, spiteful, and malicious in my soul. How polluted the stream of my spirit has become. Marah has been the waters of which I've been drinking. Today, I realize through Your word, that I've played the fool. I've felt much like Asaph and my anger has not been appropriately processed. I've taken an offense. Oh, please forgive me and heal my broken spirit.
>
> Like Asaph, let me see You again, and be near You again. Through Your precious blood, Jesus, make my heart right again with You and

Father. Holy Spirit, I HAVE GRIEVED YOU! I am so sorry. Please return to me in full measure. I can't make it without YOU. Make me pure again, put the wood of Your cross into my heart, Jesus. Let there be sweetness in my soul that will then be transferred to all of my relationships. Let me see no one but You, Jesus Christ. For in Your face I see Father.

Today, I release my "causes" to You, Sovereign Lord. I turn from my need to be right, from my stubbornness and self-rightness, from my lack of daily turning my heart over to You. You, God, are the strength of my heart.

Thank You, Father, that I belong to You and You are mine! Like Asaph, 'whom do I have in heaven but You...I desire You more than anything on earth' (I say that by faith). Today, I have made You, Sovereign LORD, my Shelter...so I rest in Your protective and providing care, under the shelter of Your wings. I release to You, Jesus Christ, my bitter heart. I am clean by Your Word and Spirit. Amen."

Chapter Four

COVENANT RELATIONSHIPS

Lydia and I got married in 1980. We were two teenagers in love; I was 19 and she was 16. As we stood there before Thomas Patterson, my father-in-law-to-be, who was the minister performing the ceremony, Lydia and I repeated vows that millions and millions of couples have said: "For better, for worse; for richer, for poorer; in sickness and in health, I promise to be faithful to you only all the days of my life, so help me God."

Our marriage covenant was more than a paper we signed, or words that we parroted. Rather it was a deep, from the heart, lifetime commitment to each other. And little did we realize on that cold and snowy February day, the full impact of those covenant vows we made that day. In the decades that have followed we certainly have experienced both better and worse, both richer and poorer, and both sickness and health.

That is a marriage covenant relationship. But it's not the only kind of covenant relationship that God wants us to have. Throughout the Bible, we see God's desire for us to have that kind of covenant relationship with our family members, our close friends, members of our community of faith, and even with God Himself. A covenant relationship is any relationship where there is binding agreement that says, "We commit in our hearts to this binding agreement and lifetime relationship. For better, for worse, for richer, for poorer, in sickness and in health, I promise to be faithful to our relationship all the days of my life, so help me God."

I believe this is the highest level of relationship we can ever experience. Don't we all crave these kinds of covenant relationships? And the reason we desire it so deeply is God put that desire in us. He wants us to have covenant friendships in every area of our lives.

This kind of covenant friend is a friend:

- Who will keep your confidences and never divulge them, even if tortured and tempted with chocolate.

- Who will quietly destroy the photograph that makes you look like a beached whale!

- Who knows you don't know what you are talking about, but will let you reach that conclusion on your own.

- Who will go on the same diet with you—and off the same diet with you.

The Proverbs describe a covenant friend this way, *"A friend loves **at all times** and a brother is born for adversity"* (Proverbs 17:17 NIV).

I love the story of General William Westmoreland in the Vietnam War when he was interviewing a whole platoon of paratroopers. "Do you love jumping?" he asked. "I love it sir," came the reply of many. Finally he came up to one guy that said, "I hate it, sir." "Then why do you do it?" he asked. "Because I love the men who jump, sir!"

Jesus loved those He "jumped" with. Listen to what He said to those who were in covenant with Him: *"I no longer call you servants, because a servant does not know his master's business. Instead, I have called you **friends**, for everything that I learned from my father I have made known to you."* (John 15:15 NIV). Just like Jesus, you can't have a lot of these covenant relationships (He only had 12 disciples in His inner circle), but you can have, and need, a few.

So how do you develop these kinds of covenant friendships in your family, in your close friendships, and in your church family? I want to show you how by looking at one of the most moving stories in the Bible about friendships.

The story begins with a man moving his wife, Naomi, and their two sons to a new country because the economy had tanked back home. Almost immediately after arriving in this new country the man suddenly dies, leaving his wife and two sons in a desperate situation. The sons soon marry two local ladies named Ruth and Orpah. All goes well for them for a decade or so, but then suddenly both of the sons tragically die, leaving their widows behind. So here is Naomi, and her two daughters-in-law in deep grief and in a real financial mess.

But then Naomi hears that the economy had turned around back home and that they could get some help there. So she and her two daughters-in-law start down the road from Moab to Bethlehem. The Bible says, *"After a short while on the road, Naomi told her two daughters-in-law, 'Go back. Go home and live with your mothers. And may God treat you as graciously as you treated your deceased husbands and me. May God give each of you a new home and a new husband!' She kissed them and they cried openly"* (Ruth 1:8-9 MSG).

What did Ruth and Orpah do at this covenant crossroad? They had been in covenant relationship with Naomi and her family, but now times are tough; all the men had died. To move forward to Bethlehem with their mother-in-law means complete uncertainty. But to go back home to Moab seems to have more future hope. Notice the two responses:

"Again they cried openly. Orpah kissed her mother-in-law good-bye; but Ruth **embraced her and held on**. *Naomi said, 'Look, your sister-in-law is going back home to live with her own people and gods; go with her.' But Ruth said, 'Don't force me to leave you; don't make me go home.* **Where you go, I go; and where you live, I'll live. Your people are my people, your God is my god; where you die, I'll die, and that's where I'll be buried, so help me God—not even death itself is going to come between us!'** *When Naomi saw that Ruth had her heart set on going with her, she gave in. And so the two of them traveled on together to Bethlehem."* (Ruth 1:14-19 MSG)

Here at the covenant crossroad Orpah cries, kisses and then leaves. But Ruth cries, clings but then refuses to go! She says, "I am going to stay in our covenant relationship!"

What can we do to nurture those kinds of covenant relationships in every area of our lives—in our homes, friendships, and church family?

The first thing I would suggest is this: _decide that you will be a "cleaver" not a "leaver."_ Orpah cries and kisses, but then leaves; Ruth commits and clings, and stays! A "kisser" is the friend who is there while things are going their way, while things are going smoothly. But when the tide turns and life gets tough, the "leaver" bails out. They break covenant and run the other way.

On the other hand, a "cleaver" is someone who, when everything is going badly in your life, stays with you. They don't leave, they cleave! The cleaver is somebody who is in your corner when you're cornered; it's somebody who is like toothpaste—they come through in a squeeze. It's somebody who comes in when the whole world has gone out. That's a cleaver, a covenant friend.

The Bible says, _"There are 'friends' who pretend to be friends, but there is a friend who **sticks closer** than a brother"_ (Proverbs 18:24 TLB). Covenant friends are "sticky" friends! They stick with you, and you stick with them, through the tough times of testing, trial, and tragedy.

When does a person need our support the most? When they've got it all together, or when they're struggling, hurting, and dying inside? When they're struggling. Haven't you seen people who got a divorce and then were ostracized by their "leaver" friends? Or folks who got into financial trouble, and then were abandoned by their "leaver" friends? Or, those who have had their children get into legal trouble, and then suddenly no one wanted anything to do with them?

What a gift it is to have someone stand by you in times of trouble, who helps carry your burdens—whether you're right or wrong. Job said: _"A despairing man should have the devotion of his friends, even though he forsakes the fear of the Almighty"_ (Job 6:14 NIV).

Are any of us perfect? No. We're going to make mistakes. Yes, sometimes stupid mistakes! At that time, more than any other, we need a loyal friend, a friend who says, "Even if you go off the deep end and turn from your faith, and run from God, and go out and mess up your life, I'm going to hang in there with you till you come to your senses." You and I don't have to endorse what others have done, but we can be there for them and with them, so that they don't have to suffer alone.

The fact is, a friendship is not a true friendship until it's a **tested** friendship. When the test came at that covenant crossroad for Naomi and her two daughters-in-law, Ruth revealed how committed she was to the covenant relationship, and Orpah revealed how uncommitted she was. The true friendship was revealed by this test.

My wife, Lydia, and I know a couple that have been our lifetime covenant, and best friends. Their names are Bill and Beth Chaney. We have been friends for right at forty years. All those years ago we made up our minds that we were going to stay in covenant "no matter what." Little did we know back then what "no matter what" would mean. Through the years we've experienced our best times and our worse times, together. Our friendship is a true friendship because it's been a tested friendship.

We have worked together, played together, and raised our families together. We've laughed, we've cried, we've fought, and we've made up. And through each passing test, our relationship has deepened and we've proven to each other that we are cleavers, not leavers.

Bill has proven again and again to be a cleaver in my life—especially when things have been hard. I remember a time, back in the early 90's, when I experienced the most difficult and challenging moment in my life up to that point. Lydia and I experienced a devastating period in our relationship that had the potential to destroy both our marriage and ministry. Lydia and I were at our wits end about what to do.

At the time, Bill was working at a church in Concord, California. The moment I called him and he heard the pain my voice he said, "James, I will be there in four hours." In that crossroads moment for Lydia and I, in the midst of our wreckage and pain, Bill came immediately and brought a sense of calm and sanity to our circumstances. He let Lydia vent and process all her anger and hurt. He let me process my emotions. And during the weeks that followed, Bill walked through our troubles with us and got us on the road to recovery. It was a turning point in our marriage, and in the life of our New Life family. Our lives have not been the same since, all because Bill was a cleaver not a leaver. When I needed him most, my covenant friend came through for me.

Whether it's in our marriages, or our relationships with our kids, or in our friendships, we must decide that we are going to be cleavers not leavers. That's the first step to experiencing true covenant relationships.

Another thing we must do is *allow the relationships to change.*

Orpah shed just as many tears and Ruth did. Her handkerchief was just as damp as Ruth's was. So what was the difference between these two women? Orpah was probably thinking, "Naomi, you've changed, I can't go with you. Things aren't like they use to be. You have no husband or sons now. You say God is with you. Really? I think I'll stay here." On the other hand, Ruth embraced the changing relationship because her covenant relationship had nothing to do with **circumstance**, it had to do with **commitment**.

But Ruth's attitude was: "Naomi, as you change I will change with you. Where you go I will go, where you stay I will stay. Your people will be my people. Your God will be my God. You and I are about to change geographically, as we go from here in Moab back to Bethlehem. We are going to change relationally, because ultimately I will remarry. But I will embrace all of the changes that God is doing in both of our lives. The only thing that won't change is our covenant relationship."

Friends give each other space and grace to change!

One of my dear covenant friends is a man in our church family by the name of Everette Claiborne. We have now been friends for over thirty years. And I have had the privilege of being his family's pastor for over 26 years. When I first became the lead pastor of New Life Center at twenty-seven years old, Everette came to me and said, "Pastor James, as you lead this church, you will have enough critics, so I feel God has called me to be your greatest encourager and leave the criticism up to others. And that's what I commit to do, I will be your friend who will be your greatest encourager."

He has kept his promise! But the only way he has been able to do that is by allowing me to grow into the person that God intended for me to become. The truth is, through the decades I have changed a lot. The church has grown from 45 weekend attenders to thousands who now call New Life their church home. And with that growth I've had to continue to develop as a person and a leader. Everette has not only allowed me to do this, he has encouraged me to! Still today he is my biggest encourager! It's one of the reasons why at both our 20th and 25th celebrations of being lead pastors at New Life, he and his wife Sue sat right next to Lydia and I.

Friends must allow friends to change!

Parents must allow their kids to change, to grow, and become what God wants them to become. I've seen it many times where a parent is still trying to control their twenty-one year old as if they were five years old. They never let them go in order to grow, and then wonder why the parent-child relationship is strained.

Spouses must allow their spouses to change from one season of life to the next. Because Lydia and I got married so young, I've watched her mature from a 16 year old, through her 20's, 30's, 40's, and now—well, I forgot, she's stuck at 49.

In those early years of our marriage I would say, "Lydia, you've changed. You're not like you to use to be." And I tried to get her to stay how she "used to be." But the fact is, she wasn't supposed to stay like she used to be. And I'm so glad that over these years I've learned to let her go, and let her grow, because she has blossomed into the most amazing woman I know!

All covenant relationships are committed to allowing one another to change.

Another thing we can do to nurture our covenant relationships is to **speak words of life**. What do I mean by words of life? First, we want to speak words that let the other person know that we are committed to them for a life-time. It's what Ruth said to Naomi, "I'm not leaving! No matter what,

I'm staying!" Just in case Naomi was somehow missing it, Ruth concluded by saying, *"May the LORD deal with me, be it ever so severely,* **if anything but death separates you and me**" (Ruth 1:17 NIV).

One of the commitments that Lydia and I made from the beginning of our marriage was to never use the "D" word—divorce. We agreed that divorce would never be an option (murder might be, but not divorce). The reason we have chosen not to allow the "D" word in our marriage is because the Bible says, "Death and life are in the power of the tongue" (Proverbs 18:21 ASV). We want to speak life-giving words not death-giving words to each other.

Speaking words of life to someone means telling them, "We are in it to win it! We're going the distance." Speaking words of life can also mean *"speaking the truth in love"* (Ephesians 4:15 ESV). A friend will say to you what needs to be said, even if it hurts a little bit. Solomon said, *"Wounds from a friend can be trusted, but an enemy multiplies kisses"* (Proverbs 27:6 NIV). What does it mean, "An enemy multiplies kisses"? It means that someone who isn't your covenant friend will say whatever is easiest to say at the time. They're the ones who will smile in your face and stab you in the back. A true friend will be honest enough to say what needs to be said. They'll love you enough to wound you.

I guess you could say that if an enemy stabs you in the back, a good friend stabs you in the front! "Wounds from a friend can be trusted."

As I mentioned previously, Bill Chaney is a covenant friend, and he and I have "wounded" each other a few times through the years. Let me tell you about a time he wounded me. It happened one day when I said to Bill, "Hey, Bill, if you had just one chance to tell me the one thing you've always wanted to tell me, but you felt like you couldn't, what would that be? You only get this one shot so make it count." He said, "Are you sure you want me to be that honest with you? I don't want to hurt your feelings, James." I said, "Let 'er fly, Bill. I can handle it. No problem." He took a deep breath and then said, "Well, James, you're not a good listener!"

I couldn't believe my ears! I thought to myself, "Me, not a good listener? You've got to be kidding!" I said, "Bill, I think you're wrong. I think I am a good listener. In fact, the next time you think I'm being a bad listener you bring it to my attention." Over the next few days, about every 2 or 3 hours he would say, "James, right there, that's what I was talking about." When I would listen with my answer running, or when I looked away while he was talking, or when I interrupted him, Bill would say, "That's what I'm talking about."

That wound by my friend exposed a big weakness in my life, and it helped me to become a better husband, father, friend, and leader.

Now, let me tell about a time I had to wound my friend, Bill. It actually was the biggest argument we've ever had. It happened around 1990 when Bill and I were serving together as pastors at New Life. Right after a 6 a.m. prayer meeting, as we were leaving, Bill pulled me aside privately and said, "James, I don't feel I'm called any longer to pastoral ministry. I'm leaving Bakersfield and going back to Texas to be a chicken farmer. Chicken farmers make a lot of money and I know I can succeed at that."

Incredulously, I looked at Bill and said, "God has not called you to be a chicken farmer. He's called you to be a shepherd-leader!" And for the next thirty minutes or so I kept giving him the ICNU talk (I see in you), telling him that God had not given him leadership and teaching gifts to go back to Texas and be a chicken farmer! We argued back and forth and the quarrel escalated to the point that we both had to walk away from it for a day or two to cool off!

I "wounded my friend" by speaking the truth in love to him. I was speaking words of life to him. And, thankfully, Bill listened to his covenant friend. Over the last few decades Bill became an impacting leader at New Life with me. But he has also gone on to be an impacting lead pastor at two different churches that, through the grace of God on his life, he has grown to more than a 1000 in weekend attendance.

In covenant relationships we speak words of life!

Another way to nurture covenant relationships is to *follow God's example*. God is a covenant-keeping God, and He shows us how to keep covenants with each other.

The Bible is a covenant book. It's broken up into the Old Testament, or Old Covenant, and the New Testament, or New Covenant. It's the big story of God's covenant agreement and relationship with His people.

First, the Old Covenant was with the Jewish nation. God considered Israel His "wife," and He has had an eternal love affair with her from the beginning. Even when she continually committed spiritual adultery, God did not give up on her. (See the book of Hosea.) He would not break covenant with Israel. And to this day God's covenant is with her.

But God, who loves the whole world, decided to establish a New Covenant with Israel, to include all the peoples of the earth. The prophet Jeremiah spoke for God and said: *"The time is coming when I will make a brand-new covenant with Israel and Judah...I will put my law within them—write it on their hearts!—and be their God. And they will be my people...I'll wipe the slate clean for each of them. I'll forget they ever sinned!"* (Jeremiah 31:31, 34 MSG).

So God sent His only Son, Jesus Christ, to earth to lay down His life on the cross. And just like the Old Covenant was sealed with the blood of sacrificial animals, so Jesus, the Lamb of God, sealed this New Covenant with His own blood.

At the Last Supper Jesus lifted the chalice of wine and said, *"This cup is the new covenant written in my blood, blood poured out for you"* (Luke 22:20 MSG). Jesus went to the cross, laid down His life, paying the price for every sin you and I will ever commit. And through Him, God made it possible that every person can come into this covenant relationship with Him.

Friend, you and I are a part of the New Testament, or covenant with God! And just like He will never give up on Israel, He will never give up on you and I, the new spiritual Israel!

Make up your mind right now that you are going to be like our covenant-keeping God. That with His help you are going to love others like God loves you. That you're going to pay the price to stay in covenant, "no matter what it takes."

There is one final powerful way to nurture your covenant relationships and that is to *focus on the long-term rewards of staying in covenant relationships.*

It's sad, but Orpah, the crying-kisser, is never heard of again after that covenant crossroad experience. She died in the land of the cursed (Moab means cursed). She never went to the land of the Living Bread (Bethlehem means house of bread). When it got hard to remain in covenant, she took off.

But Ruth went with her mother-in-law to the land of bread, and she eventually found a new husband, Boaz. From that new covenant relationship with Boaz she had a child and named him Obed. That alone is a wonderful reward for staying in covenant. But there's more to the story, because the Bible says, *"Obed was the father of Jesse. Jesse the father of David"* (Ruth 4:22 NLT). Obed would eventually become the grandfather of Israel's greatest king, King David! Ruth would be the great-grand-mother of King David. That alone is a wonderful reward for staying in covenant. But eventually Ruth became the great-great-great-great-great-great-great (28 generations from David) grandmother of the Messiah, the Lord Jesus Christ! What an honor, what a privilege, what a reward! All because she stayed in covenant with Naomi!

Lydia and I are in a season of experiencing the long-term rewards, the harvest, of staying in covenant for 35 years. Our love has never been deeper; we truly are best friends. Our sons and their wives are blessing us with grandkids, and Jim and Jonathan are succeeding in their paths of ministry and life. Our church family is vibrant and growing exponentially. And New Life continues to multiply through leaders all over the world. It is a season of harvest for Lydia and I, and I am so grateful.

Friend, whether it's with your spouse, or kids, or friends, or church family, stay the course, choose delayed gratification, don't break the covenant. If it's been broken repair it. Like Ruth and Naomi, when you come to the covenant crossroad, choose to stay in covenant and enjoy the rewards of it! You'll be glad you did!

Chapter Five

FIXING FEUDS

In the last seven days how many conflicts have you had? Any with your parents? How about your husband or wife? Your kids? In-laws? Maybe with the ex-husband or ex-wife? A co-worker or friend? If I were a betting man I would bet that you had a few. How do you deal with them? How do you resolve them? My experience is most people I know find it very difficult to deal successfully with conflict. Yet fixing our feuds is one of the greatest secrets to satisfying relationships that I know of.

Conflicts happen most with those we are closest to, so what we will look at in this chapter will be from the family's perspective. But we can apply this to all of our relationships, at home, work, school, friendships, and our Community of faith.

Because of close proximity conflict happens especially in marriages. I heard about this husband and wife who had a conflict with each other, and with a highway patrolman who pulled them over.

When officer came up to the window of his car the man says: "What's the problem officer?" The officer said, "You were going 75 miles an hour in a 55 mile an hour zone." The man said, "No sir, I was going 65." His wife said, "Oh, Harry. You were going 80." (Harry gives her a dirty look.) The officer then says, "I'm also going to give you a ticket for your broken tail light." The man said, "Broken tail light? Sir, I didn't know about a broken tail light!" Harry's wife says, "Oh Harry, you've known about that tail light for weeks." (Harry gives wife another dirty look...a little more intense this time.) The officer said, "I'm also going to give you a citation for not wearing your seat belt." The man says, "Oh, I just took it off when you were walking up to the car, sir." The wife says, "Oh, Harry, you never wear your seat belt!" Harry turns to his wife and yells, "Shut your mouth!" The officer turns to the woman and asks, "Ma'am, does your husband talk to you this way all the time?" His wife says, "No, Sir, only when he's drunk."

Conflicts are going to happen-guaranteed! And the Bible is very clear on how we are to fix our feuds.

There is a very famous Family Feud in American history that just about everyone has heard of...the feud between the Hatfields and the McCoys. Does your family ever resemble the Hatfields and the McCoys?

What you may not know is how it all started between these two families. In 1878 they had a dispute over the ownership of a hog. And that dispute led to a twelve-year war which resulted in the deaths of three Hatfields, seven McCoys, and two outsiders. This disagreement over that one hog stole twelve years and twelve lives.

Friend, the way we process conflicts in our families will determine whether there is spiritual life or spiritual death in our homes; whether we experience grace and love, or hatred and division; whether we grow together or grow apart.

Jesus Christ told us why this is so important to our families, and to all of our relationships. He said, "If a house is divided against itself, that house cannot stand" (Mark 3:25 NIV).

Our Rabbi Jesus is telling us that our house cannot stand if it is constantly divided. So let's look at what the Bible says about settling our disputes appropriately, about resolving our differences constructively, and working through our disagreements successfully

In order to discover how to "Fix Our Feuds" we're going to look to the wisdom of two "wise guys" in the Bible—King Solomon and the Apostle Paul. From Solomon's Proverbs and Paul's letter we're going to find the answers.

Let me give you a simple acrostic of the word feud to show you how we can resolve our F.E.U.D.s.

The **F.** stands for: **Focus on speaking the truth lovingly.**

Paul said, "So put away all falsehood and tell your neighbor the truth" (Ephesians 4:25 NLT). As we discussed in the previous chapter, all great relationships are built on loving truth-telling. How do we do that? One way we speak the truth in love in our relationships is to simply delay our reaction long enough to see if it's worth confronting.

Don't just fly off the handle. Have you noticed how easy it is to fly off the handle? But flying back on the handle can be difficult! So before you go and tell someone the truth take a timeout.

Solomon made this clear when he said, "A fool shows his annoyance at once, but a prudent man overlooks an insult" (Proverbs 12:16 NIV). I have been "a fool" more than once! Have you? Solomon also said, "A quick tempered man does foolish things..." (Proverbs 14:17 NIV). Have you proven that recently? Solomon also quipped, "A patient man has great understanding, but a quick tempered man displays folly" (Proverbs 14:29 NIV).

A guy who managed conflict like this was Billy Martin. You may remember Billy Martin, he was the famous baseball coach for the New York Yankees. And he was known for his nasty temper that was always getting him into trouble.

Billy Martin told about how he once went hunting in Texas with legendary baseball player, Mickey Mantle. Mickey Mantle had a friend down there in Texas who would let them hunt on his ranch. So when they reached the ranch, Mickey told Billy to wait in the car while he checked in with his friend.

Mantle went in and said hello to his friend. His friend told him to have a good time hunting. And as Mickey was walking out the door the guy said, "Hey, I have a pet mule in the barn who is going blind, and I don't have the heart to put him out of his misery. Would you shoot the mule for me?" Mickey said, "No problem." When Mickey came back to the car he pretended to be angry and got in and slammed the door. Billy Martin asked him what was wrong. Mickey said, "That guy won't let us hunt and I'm so mad at him I'm going out to his barn and shoot one of his mules!"

So Mantle drove like a maniac to the barn, and the whole time Martin is protesting, "We can't do that!" Mickey said, "You just watch me". They get to the barn and Mantle jumped out of the car with his rifle, ran inside, and shot the mule dead. Just then, he heard two more shots, and he ran back to the car and saw that Martin had taken out his rifle too. He yelled, "What are you doing, Martin?" Billy Martin, with his neck veins bulging, and his face beat red, shouted, "We'll show that son of a gun! I just killed two of his cows!"

"A quick tempered man does foolish things..." "A quick tempered man displays folly." So, let's engage our minds before we engage our mouths! Let's slow down our reaction and see if it's really worth having a feud over.

Another thing we can do to speak the truth in a loving way is to make sure I get the truth before I speak the truth. Have you ever had a conflict because you didn't have the facts straight? We all have.

I remember a few years ago when Lydia and I, and our sons, Jim and Jonathan, were at our home practicing some music, preparing for our weekend services. I know what you are thinking, "That sounds real spiritual, fun, and warm and fuzzy...you know, the FAM getting ready to worship together." But in the Ranger Family we have four very strong personalities and we all have opinions on how things ought to go.

I was at the keyboard and we were going over parts for the song. Jonathan was doing a harmony part that I didn't think fit, so I told him so. He said, "Dad, you're wrong. That is the way they do it on the recording." I knew he was dead wrong so I challenged his opinion. I said, "Jonathan, that harmony part doesn't fit this song, and we need to do it my way."

Well, then Lydia and Jim joined in and took sides with Jonathan. They both said, "I believe he's right." Now I had the whole family against me! But being the man of deep conviction, and knowing that when I'm right I have to stand up for it, I stood my ground.

Jonathan said, "Ok, dad, let's just play the original version and see who's right." I thought, "Poor Jon, he's going to make a fool out of himself." But I said, "Ok, go ahead." So Jon went and got the CD, played the song, and sure enough, it was just like he said!

I, of course, was humble and sorrowful for my wrong accusation, right? NOT! I said, "I don't care if they wrote it like that or not, it doesn't fit!" I later repented and we did it Jon's way.

No wonder Solomon had a lot to say about getting the truth before you speak the truth. *"What a shame—yes, how stupid!—to decide before knowing the facts!"* (Proverbs 18:13 TLB).

Another way we can speak the truth in love is to make a decision about what truth needs to be said. Does all truth need to be expressed? No!

For example, have you heard of the famous conflict between Winston Churchill and Lady Astor? They despised and loathed one another. And Mr. Churchill made things worse by not keeping his private thoughts private.

On one occasion Lady Astor said to Churchill, "If I were your wife I would fill your cocktail glass with poison." Churchill said, "If you were my wife, I would drink it." On another occasion, Lady Astor said, "Mr. Churchill, you are dis-gracefully drunk!" Churchill said, "Yes I am. And you, my dear lady, are disgracefully ugly. What's more, tomorrow morning I will be sober but you will still be ugly."

Sometimes it's best to keep our comments to ourselves...even if it is the way we feel, and even if we think it's the truth.

Once we decide this truth needs to be said we must, **Focus on speaking the truth lovingly**

The **E.** stands for **Express My Anger Appropriately.**

Anger is a part of our God-given emotions, and there are times we should be "Good and mad." But, as we try and resolve conflict in our relationships, there is an appropriate way, and an inappropriate way, to express our anger.

Solomon said, *"A fool gives full vent to his anger but a wise man keeps himself under control"* (Proverbs 29:11 NIV).

How do you deal with your anger when you're in a conflict with someone? We all have different techniques...and most of them don't work too well. I remember when Lydia and I first got married. Because we were so young, one of my mature ways of resolving conflict when I was upset was when we got into it late at night I would simply and abruptly get up in the middle of the argument and go to bed. I thought, "I'll show her. I'll just go to bed and pretend this disagreement isn't bothering me and she'll come groveling back on bended knees and apologize."

There's good news and bad news in this story. Good news...my method worked for the first two years. Bad news...she caught on. To my chagrin, one night after we had gotten into "a debate" I went to bed at 9 o'clock and I waited for her to come groveling to me like she always had. 9 turned into 10, 10 into 11. Finally around one in the morning I go out into the living room and there she is...fast asleep, lying there so peaceful. Now, I was sure enough ticked off! She's lying there peacefully asleep, and I'm so adrenalized I can't go to sleep! These days, after many years of marriage, it's just not worth the effort. We save our energy for the things that really matter.

Paul talked about what to do with our anger in our conflicts. He said, *"And don't sin by letting anger gain control over you. Don't let the sun go down while you are still angry, for anger gives a foothold to the Devil"* (Ephesians 4:26, 27 NLT).

In this verse Paul gives us three ways for *expressing our anger appropriately.*

1. Be angry but...**DON'T SIN.** Don't let your anger "gain control over you." Anger is a good, God-given emotion, but it must be released appropriately.

2. Be angry but...**DEAL WITH IT WITHIN 24 HOURS.** "Don't let the sun go down while you are still angry." If you do, it will lead to bitterness, and will poison your soul.

3. Be angry but...**DON'T GIVE THE DEVIL A FOOTHOLD.** When we are confronting issues in our relationships, if we let our anger get out of control, the Devil will use that to ruin our relationships and make us miserable.

So, what do you do when conflict happens and you get angry? I heard Rick Warren say it best. There are three ways to respond:

1. You can **Repress** it by denying it or just keeping it inside. But eventually it's going to be like the hot lava repressed down in the earth—it will ultimately explode out the mouth of the volcano and hurt rather than help. (Can anyone say "Passive-Aggressive"?)

2. Or you can **Express** it in an inappropriate and destructive ways.

3. Or you can **Confess** it and **Process** it. Just be honest and confess it, "I'm angry," and then you deal with it appropriately.

"A gentle answer turns away wrath, but a harsh word stirs up anger" (Proverbs 15:1 NIV). The question is, do you want to "turn away" their anger or "stir up" their anger? If you want to "turn away" or calm their anger then give a gentle answer.

If we want healthy, authentic relationships then we must express our anger appropriately.

The **U.** in the word Feud stands for **Use My Words Wisely.**

Paul said, *"Don't use foul or abusive language. Let everything you say be good and helpful, so that your words will be an encouragement to those who hear them*" (Ephesians 4:29 NLT). Notice the words, "Foul" and "Abusive." That literally means putrid, or rotten, or corrupt or harmful.

It's what Actor Alec Baldwin did to his 11 year old daughter some time ago. I'm sure Alec is a good guy, but he sure blew it on this one. You may remember the story about how, in an angry tirade that he left as a voice mail on her cell phone, Alec spewed out on his little girl many putrid, harmful and abusive words. And at the end he called her "a rude, thoughtless little pig."

What made it even worse for me was his response to the public for his harmful words. Alec said he was sorry for saying it...BUT, that he was driven to saying it. Listen, we all have said harmful things to others, but there is never an excuse for it, and when this happens we should always own our part, and apologize immediately.

I can't tell you how many times I've had to apologize to my two sons, as they were growing up, for "speaking the truth" ...but in an unloving way. As parents we can get so frustrated, worried, angry that we use our words unwisely, and it causes damage to our kids.

When we do this, if we want to keep our relationships healthy, we will go back to our kids, or our mate, or our parents, or our friends, and say, "What I said I really did mean, but how I said it was so wrong. Would you please forgive me?" Those are some very healing, and life-giving words!

Paul says we should never use words in our relationships that are "foul" or "abusive." He says, only use "good and helpful" words. Doesn't that simplify it for us? When we have conflict with others all we have to do is ask ourselves, "Am I using only good and helpful words as I confront this issue?"

"Well, James, are you saying I have to be passive about it, a panzie-wanzie?" Not at all. In fact, you need to say exactly what you think and feel, but say it **"gently and firmly."** Those two words are key, "gently and firmly." When we are in conflict with someone, we don't have to put heat on our words in order to have impact. We need to say what we need to say...gently, yet firmly. Make sure our words are good and helpful and healing.

"Reckless words pierce like a sword, but the tongue of the wise brings healing" (Proverbs 12:18 NIV).

How do we fix our feuds in our relationships? F.ocus On Speaking the Truth Lovingly. E.xpress My Anger Appropriately. U.se My Words Wisely. And the letter **D.** stands for...

Deal with the Past Quickly. Deal with your conflicts as soon as you can. Don't delay, or procrastinate. Don't say, "I'll do it later." Put away your past behaviors and hurts quickly.

Why is this so important? Because most people live in the past and never get around to the present. They spend so much time looking in their rear view mirror that they never see what wonderful things God has for them in the here and now, and in their future.

First, Paul says, deal with your **Past BEHAVIOR**. *"Get rid of all bitterness, rage, anger, harsh words, and slander, as well as all types of evil behavior"* (Ephesians 4:31 NLT). The truth is we've all hurt others in our past with our behavior. And if we don't deal with it and get rid of it we can go all the way through life living with regrets. And what good do regrets bring?

One of my favorite actors is Morgan Freeman. And he said, "You can regret all you want. But what does it change? It just causes a sore inside you that festers. Next thing you know, you're dying and you don't know why."

The good news is God doesn't want us to live one day of our lives with regrets from our past relational failures. He's made it possible for us to get rid of our regrets. How do we do that? It may mean you deciding right now to set up a time with someone you've done wrong in your past. It also may mean you humbling yourself and saying, "I was wrong, would you please forgive me?"

God wants to help us live with no regrets and put away our past behavior.

But He also wants to help you put away your **Past HURTS**. This deals with a past conflict where someone hurt you and you choose to forgive them.

Paul said, *"Be kind to each other, tenderhearted, forgiving one another, just as God through Christ has forgiven you"* (Ephesians 4:32 NLT). Whenever I talk about forgiveness in a message, inevitably, someone comes up to me and says, "But James, why should I forgive them? They hurt me, and it hurt really badly. If I forgive them then they get away with it. I'm going to make them pay for it."

That always reminds me of this little boy who sat on a park bench in obvious pain. A man walked by and asked him what was wrong, and the little guy said, "I'm sitting on a bumble bee." The man said, "Well, son, why don't you get up?" The boy said, "Because I figure that I'm hurting him more than he's hurting me!"

Maybe you are trying to handle forgiveness like this little boy. You endure the pain of past hurts, resentment, and unforgiveness…all because you believe you're hurting the other person more than they're hurting you. God wants us to make the choice to get off the bench of unforgiveness, and start enjoying the freedom of forgiveness. Then both you and your offender can begin to experience relief from the pain.

Always remember that anytime we don't forgive, and we have the "I'll show them" attitude, it hurts us more than it hurts them. Unforgiveness is like drinking the rat poisoning expecting the rat to die! That's why we must forgive and learn to let go of the past.

Some years back I had one of my dearest friends, Eddie Summers, do something that I felt was a total betrayal. It was the deepest pain my heart had ever experienced up to that point. Eddie's actions affected not only me, but more importantly everyone I loved.

Over time we both tried to resolve the issues but never could. And my heart took an offense toward him. And over a period of time I subtly got full of bitterness that I actually felt righteous about.

A few years down the road I was up at Camp Tehachapi for a day of solitude, silence and prayer. God surprised me when He revealed the unforgiveness in my heart toward Eddie. He showed me that I was trapped in my bitterness with an "I'll show him" attitude, while all along my unforgiveness was hurting only me.

On my way down from the mountain God whispered to me that I had to make things right with Eddie in order for me to move on with life to the good things He had in my future. So I picked up my phone and called Eddie and asked him to meet me at the Burger King in town. He said yes and came right over.

As we sat at that table it felt very awkward at first and we made small talk. Then I said to him, "Eddie, here's what I've done, said, and felt toward you that was wrong. Would you forgive me?" He said he would. Then I said, "Here are the things that you've done that have hurt me deeply." With tears in his eyes he said, "James, would you forgive me. I'm sorry." I said, "Yes I do."

Then, right there in that Burger King, I grabbed both of his hands to say a prayer. We both started crying. (I'm sure folks were wondering what these two fellows were doing holding hands and crying. It was a touching moment!). We both prayed a prayer of blessing over each other and our families. That prayer began a wonderful reconciliation and healing to Eddie and my relationship.

I walked away from that Burger King feeling like a million pounds had been lifted off my shoulders. And from that experience I wrote a song about forgiveness and letting go. I called it "Letting Go." Here is part of it...

The relationship, I held so dear,
All overnight, seem to disappear.
I wonder if I'll ever get through the pain?
As I hold on to the hurt inside,
The time has come for me to decide,
To hang on is loss, but to let go is gain!

I'm letting go of the things I've held on to.
Fears of my future, regrets of the past.
I'm letting go, but oh my God I'm holding on to you!
I give up control, I'm letting go. Now I'm free at last.

You say, "James, I can't do that by myself." You're right! You need a power greater than yourself. That power is found in Jesus Christ. Look at what Paul said again. He said, "Forgiving one another" How? "Just as God through Christ has forgiven you." What gives us the strength to fix our feuds, and forgive our offender, and repair our relationships? By remembering how much God has already forgiven us.

Jesus Christ came to earth to bring peace between us and others. And with His help, as we do what we've just looked at, we can fix our feuds and enjoy real peace in all of our relationships.

Chapter Six

MAKING MY DYSFUNCTIONAL RELATIONSHIPS FUNCTIONAL

What most of us want is to have real, authentic relationships where communication is free-flowing, natural, loving, kind, and honest. Although I'm not perfect at this (who is?) it is something that I'm always striving for.

But it hasn't always been like that. In fact, for the first three decades of my life, it was quite the opposite. As one of my dear friends once told me, "James, you hold your cards closer to you than anyone I've ever met."

Most of my early life, in family and religion, had shaped me to be that way, and it created a culture of secrecy. "Whatever you do, don't share your real thoughts and feelings. Don't be real about your insecurities, struggles and sins. Keep that stuff stuffed way down deep inside. If you do, you'll be safe."

In those early years, the questions, struggles, and problems that I had in my marriage, my ministry, and in my life in general, all went under the surface. I fit the description of a dysfunctional person. In fact, when I first heard this description of a dysfunctional person years ago by Dr. Henry Cloud and John Townsend, I thought, "That's me!" Cloud and Townsend say someone who is dysfunctional in their relationships...

- Doesn't talk

- Doesn't trust

- Doesn't feel

They don't talk honestly, or trust appropriately, or feel genuinely.

This dysfunction of mine all began to change in my early 30's when God started me on a journey of becoming authentic in my relationships. It came through some train-wrecks, relationally, and through some pain that forced me to come to grips with my brokenness and dysfunction. Through some wonderful Christian counselors, and my patient wife, and a few good close friends, I learned how to become functional; I learned how to talk honestly about my heart-issues, how to trust others appropriately (as they earned it), and how to express how I felt in my emotions.

One of the classic symptoms of any dysfunctional relationship is when people don't talk about real issues and how each person feels about those issues. And that kind of non-communication can destroy true intimacy, and ultimately the relationship, completely.

How do we turn those kinds of dysfunctional relationships around to become "functional"? One of the ways we can do this is learning from someone who did it wrong. And one of the most famous people to do it wrong was the great leader, King David. King David is perhaps one of the greatest leaders in all of Jewish history. He was extremely successful all his life at work and ministry, in leading the kingdom. He killed giants, overcame unbelievable adversity, conquered kingdoms, escaped assassination attempts on his life, and led Israel into one of her finest eras ever. He was successful everywhere—except at home, with his family. He and his sons and daughter had classic dysfunctional relationships. And, at times, it became severe.

David, like some of my readers, had the challenge of a blended family, having children from different wives. One day the challenge came to a head. After his children had become adults, David's son, Amnon, raped his half-sister, Tamar. It was a horrible thing that happened to his family.

And how does this godly father deal with this tragedy? He gets "very angry." That's good. But he does absolutely nothing, and says absolutely nothing. That's bad! There is no account of David ever saying anything to Amnon, Tamar, or Tamar's brother, David's other son, Absalom. There were no consequences for the young man's sin; no release for Tamar's shame and pain; and no release for Absalom's rage.

How does David's daughter feel? Betrayed! Betrayed by her half-brother, Amnon, who violated her, and betrayed by her father, David, who kept silent. Because of her father's non-action and crushing silence, this young lady carried a heavy burden for the rest of her life! The Bible says, "She lived in desolation." How sad.

I wonder how many family members are carrying unnecessary emotional burdens simply because of silence in the family. I wonder how many friendships are burdened with emotional baggage simply because some friends are not talking honestly with each other. I wonder how many work relationships are toxic simply because employees and employers aren't being honest with each other.

The good news is, relational corruption and corrosion can be stopped, and even healed when someone honestly opens up and begins to deal with the pain of the secrets. As Rick Warren says, "The revealing of feelings is the beginning of healing."

I remember when I first started to get honest about what was going on inside of me. I was 31 years old. I had so much pain in my soul that I never shared with my wife, or with my parents, or any friend. At the core of my pain was this dark secret of childhood sexual abuse by a relative that I had never told anyone about. Like most victims of sexual abuse, I carried a lot of shame, and therefore, kept it all inside.

The first person I ever opened up to was my good friend, Bill Chaney. It was the scariest moment of my life. I took him out to a restaurant and I said, "Bill, I'm going to tell you something that I've never told anyone else." (By the way, anytime someone says those words they are on their way to a major breakthrough in their life!) As I began to pour out the pain in my heart to Bill, I could not control the tears. But the tears were the beginning of my healing.

After talking to Bill I decided I was going to go see a Christian counselor. I had never been to one before. I was so untrusting, and so frightened of having the real me exposed, that when I walked into his office the very first thing I said was, "You are a professional counselor, and you are sworn to keep secret whatever I say to you. So if you ever repeat what I'm going to tell you, I'll sue you! Now, let's get started!" That counselor looked at me like, "This guy is a loon!"

But that experience with Bill and that counselor started me on a journey of honesty, and authenticity, with God, myself and others, that I am still on till this day. And it has led me down a path of wonderfully real relationships.

One of the key questions we have to ask ourselves is, "Whose responsibility is it to initiate the 'let's talk about this' conversation?" It is always the parent, the leader, the pastor, the director. Leaders lead!

King David did not do this. He led everywhere except in this area. And because David, the parent, was silent, everyone else in the family was silent. Nobody discussed the family secret. They thought about it, maybe even wished someone would expose the pain, but nobody brought it up. "Dad isn't talking about it so I guess we shouldn't either. Let's not rock the boat."

Parents, leaders, bosses, always have the responsibility to initiate the communication process in discussing difficult issues and problems. If they do, it can lead to whole and healthy relationships; if they don't it can lead to the type of relationship that David's family had—destructive, demoralizing, and damaging. One of the motivators that will keep us working at authentic and truthful relationships is to remember the consequences of staying silent.

How did this silence affect David's blended family? It created an undercurrent of all kinds of negative emotions for everyone.

- David had to be an emotional wreck dealing with guilt over Tamar and anger toward Amnon. "I should have done something to prevent this" or "I am so angry with Amnon for what he's done."

- David's wife, Maacah, Tamar's mother, dealt with some anger and bitterness toward her stepson.

- Tamar dealt with shame, fear, embarrassment, and probably rage toward her half-brother.

- Amnon could possibly have dealt with unresolved shame and guilt; or more likely he dealt with pride and arrogance, because he seemingly got away with his horrible sin.

- Absalom dealt with deep feelings of hate, resentment, and revenge!

Unresolved issues destroy the emotional wellbeing of everyone involved. That's why they must be dealt with immediately and honestly.

Now, notice that Absalom seemed to be the troubled child in this family. He's the child that was always "acting out." But could it be that he was acting out in destructive ways because his thoughts and feelings weren't being dealt with by his parents in constructive ways?

Later on down the road, when Absalom was trying to get his father's attention to confront these issues, his father wouldn't listen to him. So what does he do? He sets someone's field on fire. That got his dad's attention!

Parents, teach your kids to talk to you about what's going on inside their hearts and minds. If they seem to be "a troubled child" it may mean that they need to be "a truthful child," and tell you about what's going on inside of them. Not always, but many times the old adage is true—hurt people, hurt people. So we need to find out what the hurt is. Make it normal to have "honest to God" families. If we do that it might mean that they won't set someone's field on fire to get your attention!

Absalom didn't confront his brother after he had violated his sister, and he let his hatred get deeper and deeper. The Bible says, *"And though Absalom never spoke to Amnon about this, he hated Amnon deeply because of what he had done to his sister."* (2 Samuel 13:22 NLT)

In this dysfunctional family Absalom followed his dad's example of non-confrontation. Absalom "never spoke" to Amnon about the issue or how he felt, nor did he speak to his father about it. So what became of this unresolved anger? It turned into full-blown rage and murderous feelings!

RELATIONSHIPS DIE WHEN SILENCE LIVES!

More than likely for us, it's not murdering a person, but murdering a relationship. The relationship dies when issues are not dealt with honestly.

For "Two years..." (2 Samuel 13:23) Absalom kept this stuff inside himself. Two years! Talk about violating God's directive for dealing with our anger. *"In your anger do not sin: Do not let the sun go down while you are still angry..."* (Ephesians 4:26). Two years of angry sun-downs.

Two years of pent up fury was about to explode on the head of his brother. Two years of frightening silence was about to be shattered by the ear-deafening thunder of released rage! Two years of family denial was about to be confronted head on. Like a bottle of coke that's been vigorously shaken, and the lid is about to come off, so the lid is about to come off of Absalom's unresolved feelings.

With the help of some friends Absalom lures his unsuspecting brother—who thinks the storm has passed—into a hurricane of rage, payback and murder. In a revengeful rage Absalom kills Amnon. There lies Amnon in a pool of blood, struck down, all because of unresolved issues and feelings that could have, and should have, been taken care of a long time before.

The Bible says that *"Absalom has been plotting this ever since Amnon raped his sister Tamar"* (2 Samuel 13:32 NLT). Two years of angry silence in this dysfunctional family resulted in death. This was the product of unresolved hate and unforgiveness.

But it wasn't just the death of Amnon. It was really the death of all of their family relationships. Absalom ran away and didn't see nor talk to his father or family for three years. Their relationships torn and destroyed. That is always the sad result of unresolved issues, secrets in relationships, and non-communication.

I wonder what would have happened if David would have lovingly, yet truthfully, confronted the issues with his children way back when they first happened? Like lancing a festering boil, that would have allowed the poison to be released and healing to begin. Yes, it would have been difficult, at best, but it would have begun the restoration of their family, rather than destroying it.

After Absalom ran away and stayed gone for three years of separation from those he loved, he finally came home, all because David says he now wants to see his son. Yet when the son arrives, David again relapses back into his avoidance of the family pain and problems by giving his son the silent treatment, and refusing to see him for two more years! So now it's a total of five years of non-communication and evading issues and feelings. Here they are now, for two long years, living within a stones-throw of each other, but they don't see each other or talk to each other! Talk about a dysfunctional family!

Can you imagine living in the same neighborhood but not talking to someone because you have unresolved issues? Happens all the time in families, in workplaces, in friendships, in churches! But this is not God's plan or purpose for our relationships. He wants us to learn how to converse honestly, communicate expressively, and confront problems appropriately. The Bible says to "speak the truth in love." As we do, healing comes.

One of the reasons David didn't talk to his son for these five years is because David had partial forgiveness. He said he forgave Absalom, but he didn't do it completely. No real and complete forgiveness is given, and the dysfunction continues:

- Don't talk

- Don't trust

- Don't feel

Functional, whole relationships happen when we choose to forgive each other "as God, through Christ, has forgiven us" (Ephesians 4:32 NLT). Aren't you glad God doesn't forgive you "partially"? I sure am.

As I will be saying throughout this book, the power of forgiveness is amazing! When we are honest in our relationships and say, "Yes, that hurt me, it hurt bad. But I choose to forgive you," that releases the healing power of God in our lives like we can't imagine. Miracles happen when we forgive and we don't seek revenge.

As I mentioned earlier, when I was in my early thirty's I began to deal with an issue of sexual abuse in my childhood. I remember the day, after three years of processing this pain through counseling and prayer, that I sat at a restaurant, across the table from the person who had inflicted that pain into my life. This was one of the most difficult moments of my thirty-something years on earth. I was filled with fear and apprehension. I had worried over and over about what and how I would say what I needed to say.

My wife, Lydia, had traveled with me to support me in my quest for closure, but now she wasn't there in this restaurant for this climatic moment. We felt it would be best for me to deal with this alone.

As we sat down at the table, this person didn't have a clue that, after these decades, I was about to deal with the pain of the past. I swallowed hard and spoke through a crackling voice. "What you did to me as a young child has caused me much harm. And it as impacted my life terribly. That spider has spun some terrible webs in my life. But I want you to know that, because of Jesus Christ, I have chosen to forgive you, and I wish you healing for your own life as well." Immediately they began to sob uncontrollably and that restaurant was filled with the sound of pain, but also of relief. Years later I discovered that this person, after our meeting, went to a counselor and began to process the pain of being sexually abused when they were a child.

That encounter was one of the most healing moments of my life! I felt the burden of years of fear, shame, and pain begin to lift. I found freedom in my soul like I had never experienced before. There is power in forgiveness!

Because of David's partial forgiveness, ultimately, Absalom betrayed his father, by trying to take over the kingdom. He wanted to see David destroyed. David had to run for his life, but later, after God intervened for him, David was reinstated to the throne. But the point is, all of this is the result of a family not talking, not confronting, not dealing honestly with hurt feelings and real issues, and not moving to real and complete forgiveness.

It's important to see that in David's family there was the constant sick sequence of:

- Abuse, then…

- Family secrets, then…

- Denial, then…

- Unprocessed feelings (anger, shame, hurt, and unforgiveness), then…

- Revenge

That's the path so many relationships take, unless they stop at "secrets," and don't go into "denial." When the boogieman is let out of the closet he loses his power and control. Expose the issue to the light and it begins to go away.

The sick sequence never changed for David's family, and in the end his family experienced two sons murdered, a daughter raped and emotionally scarred for life, and the family relationships destroyed forever.

It's vital that we learn how to be functional in our relationships because the way we run our lives at home impacts every area of our life. David lived this dysfunctional way at home and he even did this with those who worked closest to him on the job. For example, Joab, the general of David's army, was told not to kill Absalom in battle (after David had been brought back to the throne), but he did it anyway. Later Joab rebuked David as he grieved over Absalom's death. David fired Joab and appointed Amasa. What did Joab do? He murdered Amasa. How did David respond to Joab? He never confronted him over this and reinstated him to his former position. Later Joab killed Abner, another one of David's generals, and David never confronted that. And even later Joab rebuked David when he took a census of the people.

In all of these issues David remained silent. But in the end David's unforgiveness and anger toward Joab, that seethed for years, turned to revenge. It happened on David's deathbed, as he told his son, Solomon, to get Joab! "Don't let him die in peace" (1 Kings 2:6 TLB).

Amazing! Here, David brings up issues that he had never spoken to Joab about. He had worked with him, warred with him, and worshipped with him. But David stayed silent for years about how he really felt about these issues.

Being dysfunctional bleeds over into every other area of our lives. If I am silent about issues and feelings at home, or, if I am verbally abusive and raging at home, it will show up in other relationships in my life, at work and with friends.

What is the solution to being dysfunctional? How do we become functional in our relationships? Do the opposite of what dysfunctional relationships do.

Instead of abuse, work toward no abuse in all relationships. Talk about what to work at "not" doing. Define what is out of bounds. Make an agreement not to hurt each other, and when we do hurt each other we are going to deal with it "before the sun goes down," as the Apostle Paul says.

Instead of secrets in our relationships, commit to "No secrets! Ever!" When there are abuses, offences, and conflicts don't repress it, but confess it. Don't stuff it, but state it clearly. Don't bury it, but bring it out into the open so that the healing power of Jesus Christ can heal it!

Instead of denial, bring clarity on what "reality" is. We won't "fake it till we make it." Instead of unprocessed feelings, encourage appropriate expression of emotions.

Instead of revenge, turn the pain over to God and let Him repay. Because we really do believe what scripture says, *Never seek revenge! God will repay* (Romans 12:19).

How honest are you in your communication of the issues and feelings in your relationships? Do you need to work on this a little? If so, I know God wants to help you get started. So look to Him for strength to do what doesn't necessarily feel good, but is good. Choose today to be "functional" in your relationships.

Never seek revenge!

God will repay.

Romans 12:19

Chapter Seven

DEVELOPING PATIENCE IN MY RELATIONSHIPS

How patient are you with others in your relationships? If you're like me then you can probably improve just a little bit in this area. I once heard that "A man without patience is like a car without brakes." If you and I don't have patience then we're out of control and our relationships are going to crash! The Bible says, *"Impatience will get you into trouble"* (Proverbs 19:2 GNT).

In the Bible the Greek word for patience means: "takes a long time to boil." How long does it take you to boil over? We talk about somebody having a short fuse; well patience means you have a long fuse. How long is your fuse?

Patience is needed in every single relationship that we have. Why? One reason is because we're all "sinners." All of us make mistakes. We all blow it, so we're going to have to be long-suffering and enduring with each other.

We see this especially true in our families. I heard about a woman who sees a father shopping with a fussy two-year-old in his grocery cart. The guy whispers, "Be patient, Billy, you can handle this, Billy. It's okay, Billy." The woman said to him, "I don't mean to interrupt your shopping, but I just had to tell you how wonderfully loving and patient you are with little Billy." The man said, "Actually, my son's name is Patrick. My name is Billy."

We're also going to need patience with each other because we're all different from each other, and those differences can create conflict. My wife Lydia says that she and I have a wonderfully weird relationship...she's wonderful and I'm weird! She was raised in Arkansas and I was raised in Minnesota. We've often said that when we married as teenagers the North and the South met and the Civil War began.

The differences between our personalities, sexes, preferences, and a thousand other things, give ample opportunity for us to practice patience with others.

Another reason we need to develop patience with others is that we're all born impatient. Some more so than others—like me. I am not a patient man! I hate to admit, but it's the truth. Patience with others is something that I've had to work on all my life. I don't come by it naturally. My mom and dad were complete opposites when it came to this issue. Mom was eternally patient with others. Dad? Well let's just say I am wired up a lot like him!

What Mac McCleary said describes me at times, "Patience is something you admire in the driver behind you and scorn in the one ahead."

Now, there are a lot of causes for our impatience. Let me list one or two. How about being interrupted by others? Don't you just hate being interrupted? Have you ever prepared a nice dinner, then sat down to enjoy it with your family and suddenly one of your family member's cell phone rings, and they pick it up and walk in the other room? How rude! Have you ever been relaxing in the bathtub or shower and someone in your family starts banging on the door? How uncaring! Have you ever been working on a deadline and some friend shows up unexpectedly? How disrespectful!

Why does God allow these things to happen? These are opportunities for our patience to grow! The Bible says, *"Is your life full of difficulties...be happy, for when the way is rough, your patience has a chance to grow"* (James 1:2-3 TLB).

You know who handled interruptions well? Jesus Christ. Remember the time children were coming to Him, interrupting all the "important" stuff He was doing? His followers got ticked off and said, "Jesus doesn't have time for little kids! Get out of here!" Jesus said, "Hey boys, chill out, I've always got time for children."

If you have, or have had, small children then you know that little ones can sure try your patience. I heard about a mother whose patience was being severely tested by her three kids, and her friend asked her, "If you had to do it all over again, would you have children?" She said, "Sure, but not the same ones!"

Another cause of our impatience are those small, continual irritants that people create. Moses experienced this. Remember how he was in the wilderness for forty years with a couple million complaining people? They constantly, for four decades straight, created annoyances for him. Finally Moses had enough, got angry, and struck the rock instead of speaking to the rock like God said. The result of his impatience? It kept him out of the Promised Land.

Some people are being kept out of the relational Promised Land because of their impatience with others when they are being exasperating by them. Let me ask you, do irritations from those in your life bring out the best in you or do they bring out the beast in you? I suggest we learn from the oyster. The oyster takes an irritation and turns it into a pearl. That takes patience.

Patience is the ability to count down before you blast off!

Another cause of our impatience with others is having to wait on folks. When our youngest son, Jonathan, was quite small he would try Lydia's patience repeatedly most mornings. It would take the kid forever to do anything because he tended to just zone out, and she would have to stay on him constantly to get to school on time. Waiting on him tried her patience tremendously. But after a few years of this frustrating daily routine her mom was out visiting us from Arkansas and, after Lydia expressed her frustration about Jonathan to her mom, Patsy said, "Lydia, that is exactly what I use to have to do with you!" All of a sudden Lydia became much more patient with our son.

Waiting on others challenges our patience. I heard about this woman whose car died at a stop sign and wouldn't start. The driver behind her honked his horn incessantly. She helped him regain some patience by walking back to his car and saying, "I can't seem to get my car started. Would you please see if you can start it while I sit here and lean on your horn?"

So, if impatience is toxic to our relationships then what can we do to develop more patience with others? Let me suggest a few ways. **One is expect others to be "human."** In other words, don't be surprised when the folks in your family, in your circle of friends, and in your Community of Faith, and in your workplace or school have bad days. We're all eccentric and totally irrational from time to time—depending on the time of day, or the time of the week, or the time of the month!

As a pastor, I know that I have two touchy times during the week, Saturday night and Monday mornings. Monday mornings I am pretty drained because of the weekends. And Saturday night I have PMS...Pre-Message Syndrome. My wife knows that and she knows she will need to be more patient with me than normal during those times.

Women have bad days and men have bad days! As my wife says this about me, "James is so temperamental—10 percent temper, 90 percent mental!" This is why we must be patient with each other in our relationships. The Bible says, *"Be patient with each other, making allowances for each other's faults because of your love"* (Ephesians 4:2 TLB).

Another way we can learn to be more patient is to learn to listen better. I'd prefer not to talk about this one because, as I mentioned earlier, I'm not the world's best listener, but I'm "learning" to do so. Much of the time

I'm listening "with my answer running." Can you relate to that? We listen outwardly, but inwardly we're already forming our opinions, arguments, responses, and rebuttals, as we wait for that person to be quiet!

The Bible says, "A man's wisdom gives him patience..." (Proverbs 19:11 NIV). And, "A patient man has great understanding..." (Proverbs 14:29 NIV). If you are a person that boils quickly, but you want to learn to boil slowly, the key is this: understanding. The more wisdom and understanding you have about that person, the more patient you'll be with them.

The opposite is also true. If I don't understand someone I won't be patient with them. In fact, if we don't understand others then we can't have a relationship with them because all relationships are based on understanding.

For example, if I understand that behind most anger is hurt, then when a person I love is angry I can look behind the anger and see the hurt and be more patient with them. How can I better understand people? By listening to them. Not just hearing, but doing what some call "empathic listening" to "feel" what they're saying.

The Bible says, "Listen before you answer. If you don't you are being stupid and insulting" (Proverbs 18:13 GNT).

Another way of learning patience in our relationships is to see things from a different perspective. We've got to learn to see things from our friend's, or spouse's, or child's or parent's point of view.

When I see things from a bigger and more expanded point of view then I will develop more patience. For example, I heard recently about a department store manager who noticed a young boy staring intently at the handrail of an escalator. He said, "Son, are you all right?" The little boy nodded yes without looking up.

The store manager said, "Well, young man, do you want me to explain to you how escalators work?" The little boy said, "No, mister. I'm just waiting for my bubble gum to come back!" He knew something the store manager didn't and it gave him patience.

Steven Covey, author of *7 Habits of Highly Effective People*, says that one of the great habits of effective people is that they, "Seek first to understand before being understood." In Covey's book, he tells a story of when he rode the New York subway. While he was on this subway a man and his children boarded the quiet car and immediately the children started running, shouting and grabbing the passengers' possessions. The man, however, sat with his eyes closed ignoring his children. Covey became irritated until he couldn't stand it any more, so he bluntly asked the father to control his children's behavior. The man said, "Sir, I am so sorry, I just came from the hospital where my wife has just died and I just don't know what to do."

What was the result of this new information that Mr. Covey got? He says, "I saw things differently, I thought differently, I felt differently, I behaved differently." When we truly take the time to understand a different and bigger perspective of where the other person is coming from, we will be more patient.

As the Bible says, patience starts with wisdom. And what is wisdom? Wisdom is seeing life from God's point of view. It is seeing the big picture. If you want to be patient with your child, or your spouse, or your friend, then you've got to get a bigger perspective. The Bible says, *"A patient man has great understanding, but a quick-tempered man displays his folly"* (Proverbs 14:29 NIV). (I won't even ask if you've ever displayed folly because of misunderstandings!)

Another way to develop more patience in your relationships is to ask God for more of His love. In other words, learn to love others with patient love the same way God loves me with patient love.

The Bible says, *"Love is patient..."* (1 Corinthians 13:4 NIV). If that is true, then what does it mean when I'm being impatient? It means I'm being unloving.

When I'm being patient with my kids or my spouse, I'm being loving. When I'm patient with my friends, I'm being loving. When I'm being patient with those I work with, I'm being loving! But when I'm being impatient with them, then I'm being unloving.

A theme throughout this book is this: I can only give what I've received. So the key is to experience the love and patience of God first in my own life, then I will be able to give it to others. The Apostle Paul said, *"I was shown mercy so that in me, the worst of sinners, Christ Jesus might display His unlimited patience"* (1 Timothy 1:16 NIV). You'll never have to be more patient with anybody else than God has already been with you! Paul was a murderer and a religious terrorist, yet God turned him around and showed him mercy. And how did Paul respond to God's patience and mercy? He showed the world just how patient God is with us, that He has "unlimited patience"! And then Paul gave the same loving patience that he himself had received from God to people very different from himself—the non-Jews.

Jesus said, *"Always treat others as you would like them to treat you"* (Matthew 7:12 NJB). Some call this the "Golden Rule." If you want to be treated with loving patience, then treat others with loving patience. But you can't treat them that way unless you've first experienced the loving patience of our Heavenly Father.

There is one last way you and I can become more patient and that is to depend on God's Spirit for help. Honestly, if you and I try to be more patient with each other without the help of God we will be constantly frustrated, because without God's Spirit empowering us we cannot do this consistently.

The Bible says, *"We also pray that you will be strengthened with all his glorious power so you will have all the endurance and patience you need. May you be filled with joy"* (Colossians 1:11 NLT). God's Spirit in you will give you the "endurance, patience and joy" that you need to live well with those in your life. The Bible also says, *"The Holy Spirit produces this kind of fruit in our lives: love, joy, peace, patience..."* Who produces the fruit or the actions of patience? The Holy Spirit.

When you read the Bible you see that it is full of examples of people who had to rely on the power of God in order to learn to wait patiently. Noah waited 120 years before the boat started floating. (And you think you get impatient waiting for a parking space. Noah waited six months for a parking space.) Are you waiting for a marriage to get off the ground; or a friendship to turn around; or a child to change their ways? God's Spirit will help you wait.

Abraham waited ninety years before the promised son was given to him. Is God asking you to be patient before you receive a promise that He's made to you concerning a relationship? His power is within you to help you wait. Moses waited forty years in the wilderness. Maybe you feel you're in a relational wilderness, waiting for it to change, waiting for life to spring forth. And maybe it feels like it's already been forty years. God's Spirit will help you to continue waiting patiently until that relationship is restored.

All of God's great people have had to learn to wait. You will too. You will have to wait patiently for that wayward son or daughter to come to their senses, or for your husband or wife to work through the process they're in right now, or for your friend to come back around, or for that relationship to heal and recover.

What will give you patience to keep waiting is the promise of God through the prophet Zechariah, *"It is not by force nor by strength, but by my Spirit, says the LORD of Heaven's Armies"* (Zechariah 4:6 NLT).

Always remember, God's timetable is not our timetable. Be patient and wait, for as my friend Rick Warren says, **"God's delays are not God's denials!"** God our Father is all-wise and all-knowing and He has a purpose behind everything He does.

Two thousand years ago Jesus made us a promise. He said, *"But you must not forget this one thing, dear friends: A day is like a thousand years to the Lord, and a thousand years is like a day. The Lord isn't really being slow about his promise [to return], as some people think. No, he is being patient for your sake. He does not want anyone to be destroyed, but wants everyone to repent"* (2 Peter 3:8-9 NLT).

What's Jesus waiting for? He's waiting patiently for our wayward sons and daughters, husbands and wives, friends and loved ones to turn to God. He's waiting for them to experience His love and forgiveness. But one day, after that last person has come into His family, Jesus Christ will come back to this earth again, just like He said He would.

What's His motivation in waiting? Love. Because of love He is patiently waiting for just one more person to come home to the Father's house.

I encourage you to let God's love be the driving force in your life that causes you to be more patient with others. If you do this you're going to see the favor of God on those relationships!

"But you must not forget this one thing, dear friends: A day is like a thousand years to the Lord, and a thousand years is like a day. The Lord isn't really being slow about his promise, as some people think. No, he is being patient for your sake. He does not want anyone
to be destroyed, but wants everyone to repent."

2 Peter 3:8-9 NLT

Chapter Eight

BRINGING OUT THE BEST IN OTHERS

One of the most significant needs we all have is other people who bring out the best in us. And that is the very thing others want us to bring out in them...the best! Whether you're a parent, a friend, a pastor, an employer, one of the greatest gifts we can give to others is the gift of bringing out the best in them.

I remember one of the first people to ever do this in my life. His name was Mr. Johnson, my Jr. High School music teacher. I was one of those very quiet and introverted boys in school, so it's no surprise that in Mr. Johnson's class I sat in the back of the classroom, so as not to be noticed. But as that school year began Mr. Johnson did notice me. He saw something in me that I did not see in myself; an ability to create music.

One day he told all of us students to get out a piece of paper and then he told us that each one of us were going to write a song. He instructed us on how to craft lyrics, and then said, "Now, go for it."

The next day, at the end of class, he called me up to his desk. I thought I was in trouble. He pulled out my lyrics and said, "Jimmy (that's what I was called back before I matured into 'James'), out of all the papers turned in yesterday yours is the best. You really do have an ability to write songs. I hope you will develop it."

I could not believe my ears! What was birthed in my young spirit at that moment is hard to describe, but it isn't hard to see the results. It wasn't long until I wrote my first song, "Jesus Open the Windows of Heaven." That was over 300 songs ago. And I've been very fortunate to have many of my songs recorded by others. But where did it all begin? Mr. Johnson bringing out the best in me.

Henry Ford said, "My best friend is the one who brings out the best in me."

There's a man in the Bible who also did this very well. We all know him as the stepfather of Jesus Christ, Joseph. Joe had this profound ability to believe the best in his wife, Mary; to believe in her under some very difficult circumstances.

But have you ever thought about how Joseph also believed in the special child he was given to raise by God? As a "borrowed daddy," he believed in and took good care of little Jesus, even though the baby wasn't his child.

Joseph was the perfect man for the job because he knew how to bring out the best in others by believing the best in them.

I'm convinced that what the people closest to us most need from us is the very same thing. This is why the Bible makes it clear that this is what we're to do for each other. *"In response to all he has done for us, let us outdo each other in being helpful and kind to each other and in doing good"* (Hebrews 10:24 TLB).

How do we "outdo each other in being helpful," in encouraging each other, in believing the best in each other? Let's let the borrowed daddy of Jesus Christ show us to:

HOW TO BRING OUT THE BEST IN OTHERS

The first thing I want to suggest is *be a person of character.*
Joseph was a man of deep character, and his character was tested severely when he found out that his fiancé, Mary, was pregnant with a child that wasn't his. And, in fact, she was claiming that the Father was God and that

she was still a virgin! I'm sure someone was thinking, "Hey, Joe, how are you going to respond to her outrageous claims?"

Joseph agonized over what he should do. Any man would. Most men would have responded with shock. Joseph thought that Mary was a virgin. A lot of men would have responded with deep sorrow. His dreams of marriage to this young girl now seemed to be forever shattered. And a lot of men would have responded with anger. Joseph must have felt betrayed. Most men would have been looking for someone to hurt!

The fact is, by law he could have had Mary killed for what she'd done. But in the end, because he was a man of character, he decided to do the right thing. The Bible says, *"Joseph, her fiancé, was a good man and did not want to disgrace her publicly, so he decided to break the engagement quietly..."* (Matthew 1:19 NLT). Joseph was "a just man." That means he was a principle-centered man of character. Instead of embarrassing, shaming, and humiliating her, he decided to break off the engagement quietly.

What was Joseph's motivation? In the next verse it says, he did this so as not to disgrace her.

Joseph's godly character enabled him to rein in his anger. His love for Mary, even under these circumstances, compelled him to seek a way to protect her. "Love covers over a multitude of sins!"

Joseph was an unusual man. The kind of man every child wishes for: a father who knows the right way to live and who follows the right way no matter what the cost! You want to bring out the best in those you love? Be a person of character.

Another way to bring out the best in others is to *do what I call the "I see in you" technique.* It's when you can see in the other person what they may not see in themselves, or you can see in them what they are not very confident of, and you simply affirm in them what that is.

It's what Father God did to Mary when He said, "Mary, I see in you the perfect person to be the mother of my Son. It's in you. You can do this!" Because she is so young, inexperienced, and not qualified to be the "Mother-of-God," she responded with, "Who me? You've got to be kidding!" And God was like, "Yes, you!"

Joseph also did that for Mary. Once the angel confirmed that the Baby was truly God's Son, from that point forward Joseph continually affirmed that he saw in her all that it would take to be the mother of God's Son. He saw it even when others did not.

This is a powerful way to bring out the best in others and to build your relationship with them. Isn't it true that we all want someone who believes in us, and calls forth the best in us? Aren't we drawn to them? You bet!

The "I see in you" is what Mr. Johnson did for me as a young boy, that I referred to earlier. It's what so many people have done for me throughout my life. When I was around thirteen or so my dad told me something similar to what Mr. Johnson had told me. He said, "James, God has gifted you to write music that is going to be heard all around the world one of these days." My dad saw in me what I didn't see in myself at that time. It was "prophetic," in the truest sense of the word. He called it forth.

I remember when I had just graduated from High School and I was first starting to do public speaking, I was so insecure and scared. I felt totally inadequate, and not gifted to do this. And because of this I, in fact, did not want to do public speaking, but I knew that this is what God had called me to do. When I was 19 I was in a little town called Hoxie, Arkansas speaking for a church there. I had something happen to me that began to give me hope and courage that I could be a good public speaker. It's when a very old man came up to me after one of the services and said to me, "Young man, you have one of finest speaking voices I have ever heard. And I believe God is going to use you to change many lives through your speaking." I couldn't believe what he was saying! But yet his words planted a seed in my heart that gave birth to a confidence that maybe, just maybe, I can do this.

Because folks have done this in my life over and over it's probably why I get the biggest joy from bringing out the best in others by saying to them, "I see in you." I have had the joy of doing this with my wife, Lydia. She is not only a phenomenal vocalist, she is an impacting spiritual leader and public speaker. But she hasn't always been a fantastic speaker. Years back when she just started to develop her gift of communication, she would get up on

Sunday and wring her little hands so much I would fear she was going to lose them! She lacked confidence—which most new communicators do. And every week, we'd get together after the weekend gatherings—after she had spoken—and I would tell her, "Honey, you can do this! You have the gift to speak within you." Week after week I would simply encourage her to keep doing what Jesus was clearly doing in and through her life. And over time Lydia began to gain a few wins, and then that God-given confidence began to snowball, and now she is one of New Life's main communicators! But it didn't end there because now her speaking gift, along with her singing gift, goes out far beyond our local church. Lydia has ministered all over the world.

It has been my pure pleasure and joy to watch her develop and nurture that gift and watch as it blossomed and transformed lives.

Throughout my life I've done this thousands of times in the lives of my sons, and friends, and in the lives of people I've mentored. And I have to say, to do the "I see in you," and then watch it bring out the best in others, gives me more pleasure than just about anything I know!

Another way to bring out the best in others is _Develop an "Other-Centered" Attitude._ It's what Joseph did. The Bible says that, _"Joseph...determined to take care of things quietly so Mary would not be disgraced"_ (Matthew 1:19 MSG).

Do you notice how Joseph was truly concerned about the wellbeing of Mary? He didn't think, "Well, what are the boys in the neighborhood going to think about me now?" or "She has hurt me so bad I'm going to get even no matter what it takes."

No, Joseph didn't react that way. Why? Because he was "other-centered" instead of self-centered.

He was considerate of how this whole thing was going to affect Mary, more than himself. We have to remember that Joseph did this in a culture where women were no better than animals, or a piece of furniture. He could have divorced her or killed her and everyone in the village would have gone along with it. But instead, Joseph looked for ways to bring out the best in Mary in this very bad situation.

The fact is, when people are in a very bad situation that's when they need us to believe in them, and stand with them, the most. Sometimes that's when we can bring the best out of them. It takes an other-centered attitude to do this.

One of the joys of my life these days is in my relationships with young emerging leaders. And I've noticed that the times I seem to bring the best out of them the most isn't when they're doing everything right, with a sting of unbroken successes. It's when they've messed up and I come along beside them and say, "I know you're better than that. I still believe in you. Learn from your mistake, let it go and move on." Most of us never forget when someone does that for us, and it causes us to soar to the next level rather than descend into the abyss.

To truly help those in our family, our workplace, or our school we must be other-centered, and ask, "How can I best serve them? What's best for them, not me?" That's being like Jesus Christ. Did Jesus come to earth that first Christmas for His benefit or ours? Ours. Did Jesus come to earth to get or to give? To give! Did Jesus come to earth to be other-centered or self-centered? Other-centered. To bring the best out of others I must be willing to put others before myself.

Sometimes the best way to learn how to be a certain way is to look at the antithesis of what that is. And the opposite of an other-centered person, who was a self-centered person, who brought out the worst in others, was Saddam Hussein, the leader of Iraq for two decades.

In 2002, I read a Reader's Digest article that was called "The Mind of a Monster." And as I read this article I was amazed at this dictator's self-centeredness.

But I was also surprised that Saddam didn't start out that way. Did you know that Saddam grew up in a poor village in north central Iraq? And in the late 50's he joined a political party that had some very noble goals of seeking a better life for the Iraqi people.

To most, Saddam seemed to be a leader who cared for others, who was other-centered. But that all changed on July 22, 1979. In Baghdad he gathered together hundreds of members from different political parties. And he slowly strolled up to the lectern in his military uniform and then preceded to point out 60 men who he said were traitors.

Even though he had concocted the accusations, 22 of the 60 men were executed on the spot. And with that bloodbath began his reign of terror.

In 1988 he became threatened by some of his countrymen called the Kurds. So what does Saddam do? He sends clouds of poisonous gas down on them and over 5000 die—including many women and children.

Now listen to what this article said about this self-centered man: "The root of Saddam's bloody, single-minded pursuit of power appears to be simple vanity. He most wants to be admired, remembered and revered." (Reader's Digest, P.116, Aug. 2002.)

I must choose to be other-centered instead of self-centered in all of my relationships. Other-centered will bring out the best in them; self-centered will bring out the worst in them.

You say, "Well, James, if I am other-centered that sounds like I lose and they win." Not true, because in the long run their win is your win. You benefit from their self-improvement. It's not why you do it, but it is a by-product.

Did Joseph win in the long run? You bet! How would most men like to be known as the borrowed daddy of God for all eternity? What an honor Joe will enjoy forever!

Here's what it means to be "other-centered." The Bible says, "Let us have real warm affection for one another as between brothers, and a willingness to let the other man have the credit" (Romans 12:10 Ph).

Another way to bring out the best in others is to *Stay Sensitive to God's Leadings.* God will help you to see how to best help others. Notice Joseph's sensitivity to God's leadings. The Bible says, *"As he considered this, an angel of the Lord appeared to him in a dream. 'Joseph, son of David,' the* *angel said, 'do not be afraid to take Mary as your wife. For the child within her was conceived by the Holy Spirit. And she will have a son, and you are to name him Jesus, for he will save his people from their sins'"* (Matthew 1:20-21 NLT).

For Joseph, it was hard to stay sensitive to God's leadings because he had already made his plans. Have you ever made plans for yourself, or those you love, and then suddenly you get some kind of leading from the Holy Spirit that this is not what God wants for you or them? That's frustrating!

It was also hard to be sensitive to God because God's plan didn't make any sense to Joseph. Can you imagine how Joseph felt when this angel showed up and said, "Hey Joe, she's pregnant all right, but she hasn't been with any man. God did it!"?

Sometimes God's plan runs contrary to nature, to the way we've always done things, to our traditions. Joseph could have said, "Wait a minute, this can't be God because it has never happened like this before! I mean, who's ever heard of a virgin having a baby?"

When you look at Joseph's life, it's amazing how obedient he was to God's leadings, especially when most of those leadings didn't make sense. When God spoke to Joseph to marry his pregnant fiancé anyway, he obeyed, even when it didn't make sense. When God spoke to him to leave all comfort and security behind, and flee with his new family to Egypt, he obeyed, even when it didn't make sense. When God spoke to him return to Israel, after the death of Herod, he obeyed, even when it didn't make sense.

Let me say a word to parents, especially parents of adult children. I believe it is vitally important that your kids know that you believe in them and support them as they're discovering God's leadings and plans for their lives.

As far as we know Joseph and Mary, who are thought to have been in their late teens in this story, didn't have that kind of support from their families.

I know what it meant to me, when I was 23 and wife, Lydia, was 20, and we were about to move 1700 miles from Arkansas to California, to have my mother-in-law and father-in-law tell us that they believed in us, even if they didn't fully understand what God was up to in our lives.

The Spirit's leading was for me to bring my 20 year old wife, and 1 year old son, Jim, and my unborn son, Jonathan (who was still in the oven), to a place we had not been to, to a people we did not know, to a task we were unprepared for.

But, even though the plan didn't make a lot of sense at the time to Thomas and Pat Patterson (after they had given us lots of advice) they said to me, "James, we believe in you and Lydia, and we believe that God is going with you and He will guide each step of the way. Go with God's blessing." Do you have any idea what that did for Lydia and me? It gave us a lot of confidence to move into our destiny.

Parents, believe in your kids, even when it seems they're making all the wrong decisions (remember, you've made your fair share too, and lived to tell about it). Believe in your kids even when it doesn't seem they're worth believing in at the time. Believe in them even when what they're saying is God's plan for their life doesn't make a lot of sense to you. You may be right; but you may be wrong. In either case they desperately need your support, your belief in them.

Another powerful way to bring out the best in others is to Seek the Honor of God. The Bible says, *"When Joseph awoke, he did as the angel commanded and brought Mary home to be his wife, but she remained a virgin until her Son was born; and Joseph named him 'Jesus'"* (Matthew 1:24-25 NLT).

"She remained a virgin" because Joseph was a man of honor, who sought the honor of God, and what was best for Mary, not himself. Now, did Joseph have a legitimate right to have sex with Mary? Yes, because she was now his wife. But he didn't do that until after Jesus was born. Why? Because what was at stake was the honor of God. God's promise of a virgin birth of the Messiah could only happen if Joe behaved himself! And he did.

But we must remember that Joseph was a normal young man with normal sexual urges. Can you picture him, just him and Mary all alone, traveling the countryside all by themselves, for months at a time, and they're legally married. Do you think Joe was tempted along the way to say, "Mary, maybe just this once, nobody will ever know"? You bet! But because he loved God and loved Mary, and was seeking the honor of God, that gave him the courage to say no!

Love does what's best for the other person, to bring the best out in them.

Sometimes a single lady will have a guy say to them, "If you love me you'll have sex with me." The truth is, that isn't love, that's lust! Love is about giving; lust is about taking. Love is being concerned with the well-being of the other person; lust is all about me.

Like Joseph, sometimes love is about saying "no" or "wait" to our sexual urges.

The Bible says, *"Those who indulge in sexual sin...who worship idols... commit adultery...are male prostitutes...practice homosexuality...none of these will have a share in the Kingdom of God....God bought you with a high price. So you must honor God with your body"* (1 Corinthians 6:9, 10, 20 NLT).

By saying no to sexual temptation Joseph honored Mary and he honored God with his body. And so do we.

Now, obviously, Joe and Mary got to enjoy a beautiful sexual relationship later, because Jesus did have some half brothers and sisters who Joseph fathered. The stork didn't bring them; no immaculate conceptions there.

Sex is God's gift to us human beings, and within marriage it is to be enjoyed, and within marriage we actually honor God with our sexuality. But, sex outside of marriage dishonors God and dishonors the other person, and it brings out the worst in others, not the best! So, like Joseph, let's have the moral courage to honor God with our bodies.

What's the motivation for bringing out the best in others?
Love. If we love each other like Joseph loved Mary; if we love God like Joseph loved God, then we will believe the best about each other and bring out the best in each other.

Can you imagine how Mary must have felt when Joseph finally said to her, "Mary, I love you, I believe what you've said, and I believe in you. And because I love you and believe in you, I'm always going to be there to support you."?

Don't you crave that kind of love, support, and being believed in? Sure, we all do! Jesus said that when we do that for each other we're being just like Him, because that's how He treats us. Jesus said, "*Love one another. In the same way I loved you, you love one another. This is how everyone will recognize that you are my disciples—when they see the love you have for each other*" (John 13:34-5 MSG). God is honored and Jesus is glorified, when we love each other, support each other, and when we believe in, and bring out the best in each other.

Let me give you the most powerful description of love ever composed in all of literature. This describes the kind of love Joseph had for Mary, the kind of love God has for you, and the kind of love that all of us want more of. It's the kind of love that brings out the best in others.

"*Love never gives up.*
Love cares more for others than for self.
Love doesn't want what it doesn't have.
Love doesn't strut,
Doesn't have a swelled head,
Doesn't force itself on others,
Isn't always "me first,"
Doesn't fly off the handle,
Doesn't keep score of the sins of others,
Doesn't revel when others grovel,
Takes pleasure in the flowering of truth,
Puts up with anything,
Trusts God always,
Always looks for the best,
Never looks back,
But keeps going to the end.
Love never dies." (1 Corinthians 13:4-8 MSG)

How are you doing at bringing out the best in those closest to you? Do you really express your belief in them? What has God whispered to your heart while you were reading this chapter, concerning some areas He'd like you to improve in?

- Are you a person of character?
- Do you do the "I see in You" with those closest to you?
- Do you have more of an "other-centered" attitude or more of a self-centered attitude?
- How sensitive are you to God's leadings for your life and those around you?
- Parents, do your kids, no matter their age, feel your belief in them and support of them?
- Are you seeking the Honor of God in how you relate to others?

Love is the key. Why don't you ask God to make you more like Him, more loving, supporting, and believing in others? If you do, you just wait, you just watch, you are going to see God use you in awesome ways to bring out the best in others!

Chapter Nine

PERSONAL SECURITY

THE KEY TO ALL RELATIONSHIPS

In this chapter, I want to give you one of the most foundational needs of all great relationships—your personal security. Nothing will sabotage relationships quicker than our personal insecurities. If I don't feel good about myself, then how will I treat others? Not so good! On the other hand, nothing can enrich our relationships like our personal security and proper self-love. Jesus made it clear that I can only love my neighbor (or wife, husband, friend, or child) as I love myself.

I remember when I was a young pastor, how I dealt with insecurities. Because of some brokenness from my past, I was insecure about a lot of things. I was insecure about my looks, my training and preparation for ministry, not-measuring up to others, and many other things.

And how did that impact my relationships? It sometimes kept me from moving toward others to begin or deepen a relationship; it kept me from achieving the dreams God placed in my heart, and from helping others to achieve their dreams; and it kept me from empowering others, because an insecure leader can't, and won't, do that.

In my early thirties, I was introduced to a man by the name of Dr. John Maxwell who helped me tremendously to turn this all around. And that turn around began with identifying what the symptoms of insecurity are. John had a list of symptoms of insecurity that helped me. Let's look at them.

COMPARISON

We can always tell when we start to feel insecure because we start comparing ourselves with others.

I can relate. There was a time when, because of my insecurities, I had a bad habit of comparing myself with other leaders. The problem with that is, if I perceive that someone is not doing as well as I am, I can get puffed up with pride; or if I perceive that someone is doing better than I am, I can sink low into depression.

COMPENSATION

This is when we start feeling like a victim and attempt to compensate for our losses by scheming to get ahead to gain recognition, or by fighting irrational battles to get what we think we deserve.

COMPETITION

Now, there is a healthy competitive spirit, and there is an unhealthy one. An unhealthy competitive spirit is driven to outdo everyone else to get attention and rewards.

This is what Tonya Hardin did during the Olympic Games in 1994. Tonya thought to herself, "If I cannot beat Nancy Kerrigan with my talent on the ice rink, then I'll have her leg broken with a club here in the dressing room, so she can't skate. One way or another I'll beat her!" And that's just what she did. Insecurity was at the heart of Tonya's unhealthy competitive spirit.

COMPULSION

This is when, because of insecurity, I'm compulsively driven to perform to gain someone's approval. Some call this co-dependency.

This was one of the symptoms that let me know I was living and leading out of my insecurities, because I was truly a co-dependent leader. And I experienced a big downside to co-dependency and compulsion, and it's that it can lead to perfectionism, burn-out, and unrealistic expectations.

CONDEMNATION

Because of my insecurities in those early days, I tended to be judgmental toward others and myself. What's the result of that? We give in to self-pity or conceit.

CONTROL

Wow, did I ever struggle with this one. This is when feelings of insecurity cause people to validate their self-worth by taking charge inappropriately, and trying to protect their interests by monopolizing situations.

I'm sure that we can all see ourselves in at least a few of the six symptoms of insecurities. So, how do we overcome the personal insecurities that damage our relationships? What will be the source of our personal confidence?

I want to share with you a life-changing discovery I made years ago that has been the key to my personal security ever since. Yes, I still struggle with insecurities from time to time, just like all people do, but over these last two decades my personal security has become more and more strong as I've sought to live out this truth. And so can you.

Here it is: the secret of our personal security flows from the most important relationship we will ever have, and that is from our relationship with Father God through Jesus Christ. The fact is, our personal security in life will be based on our identification as God's child; that God is our loving Father and we are His kids. That experience gives us confidence to be who God made you to be, and the confidence and energy to love others and to be loved by others.

Now, the person who shows us how to do this is God's Son, Jesus Christ. Only through the life of Jesus of Nazareth can we develop that kind of personal security, and discover how it can impact our relationships and our lives.

Think of it, no person ever loved like this *man* loved. No person ever had such deep and fulfilling relationships as this *man* had. And no person has ever had such a profound sense of personal security as this *man* had.

So what was the source of Jesus of Nazareth's inner confidence? The secret is found at His baptism. Before He ever healed one sick person, exorcised one demon, or performed one miracle, He established His personal identity and security. The Bible says, *"After his baptism, as Jesus came up out of the water, the heavens were opened and he saw the Spirit of God descending like a dove and settling on him. And a voice from heaven said, 'This is my dearly loved Son, who brings me great joy'"* (Matthew 3:16-17 NLT).

In author Brennen Manning's book, "The Importance of Being Foolish," Manning writes, "When Jesus received the baptism of John at the Jordan River, he had a core identity experience...that he was **Son-Servant-Beloved of the Father.**" From that moment on, at every crossroad of Jesus' life and ministry, He constantly referred back to his identification as Son-Servant-Beloved of the Father. That was the secret of His security that gave Him confidence to face life, and the confidence to empower and love others.

That can be the source of our personal security as well—that, because of our faith in Christ, our core identity is now "I am the Father's **child-servant-beloved**." Because we have been "baptized into Christ" we all have a new identity. The Bible says, *"You are all sons of God through faith in Christ Jesus, for all of you who were baptized into Christ have clothed yourselves with Christ"* (Galatians 3:26-27 NIV). When you put your trust in

Jesus Christ as your Savior then your past life is now buried with Christ. You have been, what Jesus called, "born again."

You have a new identity! The Bible says, *"If anyone is in Christ, he is a new creation; the old has gone, the new has come"* (2 Corinthians 5:17 NIV). What does "new creation" mean? An improved version of the original? No, "new creation" literally means "a new species of being that has never existed on earth before." That means it doesn't matter what your life was B.C.— before Christ, you now have a new identity.

Let's break down those three parts of your identity. First, **you are Abba's child.** Abba, that's what Jesus called God all the time, and it was radical for Him to do so. Abba is a colloquial word used by little Jewish children when they'd talk to their fathers. And it's much more intimate than just "father." Abba literally means Papa or Daddy (or even Da Da).

Did you know that calling God Father, or Abba is something that is unique to the faith of Christ-followers? All other world religions would think it unthinkable to address Almighty God as Abba. The Abba experience is one of the greatest treasures Jesus brought us.

How secure does that make you feel when you see yourself as Abba's child, special to Him, and that He's crazy about you?

There was a little girl standing by the window during a terrible thunderstorm, and every time the lightning flashed she'd smile. Her perplexed daddy said, "Honey, what are you doing?" The little girl said, "I think that God is trying to take my picture!"

Abba is crazy about you; He probably carries a picture of you in His wallet!

The Bible says, *"…those who are led by the Spirit of God are sons of God… you received the Spirit of sonship. And by him we cry, 'Abba, Father'"* (Romans 8:14, 15 NIV).

You're not only Abba's Child, you are **Abba's servant.** You are serving Father God whenever you serve others in your home, your work, your community, or your church family. The Bible says, *"Whatever you do, work at it with all your heart, as working for the Lord..."* (Colossians 3:23 NIV). Your gracious and loving Father sees all that you do, even when others do not. And He promises to reward you both in this life and in the life to come for being Abba's servant.

You are Abba's child, and Abba's servant, but you are also **Abba's beloved.** Let me ask you, do you ever really think of yourself as God's beloved? Do you ever get up in the morning and think, "Because of my relationship with God's Son, Jesus, God loves me without limits, conditions, or strings attached?"

Do you ever think to yourself, "I am the one Jesus loves"? The Apostle John did. In fact, four times in John's gospel he refers to himself as "The disciple Jesus loved." If you were to ask John, "What is your primary identity?," he would not tell you, "I am a disciple, an apostle, or an evangelist," but he'd say, "I am the one Jesus loves."

The moment that I experience in my heart and mind that I am Abba's child and He loves me with crazy-love, that is the moment I am empowered to love others the same way! As we are saying throughout this book, you and I can only give away what we have received. Jesus said, *"Love each other. Just as I have loved you, you should love each other"* (John 13:34 NLT). When we receive Abba's love then we can give away that same love to others.

Now that we see what our identity is, let's move into how this new identity as Abba's "child-servant-beloved" plays out in our lives and relationships. Knowing your personal security "in Christ" helps you to do three things.

STAND STRONG WHEN TEMPTED

First, knowing your personal security "In Christ" helps you to stand strong when tempted. Temptation, when withstood, can give life to our relationships. Temptation, when given into, can destroy our relationships. Just ask anyone who's given in to the temptation to cheat on their spouse, or to lie, or to give in to drugs or alcohol abuse.

Our security in our identity helps us stand strong against temptation and not give in. But what happens when we forget that we are Abba's child, and that He cares for us, and wants what's best for us? We can go to some pretty dark places.

I have a friend whom I will call "Greta," who experienced a tragedy some time ago. Her mother, who she loved deeply, was in her late 40's when she passed away from cancer. Even though Greta had been a Christ-follower all of her life, this tragedy threw her into a tailspin about her faith. Here's what she told me, "After my mom died from cancer I was so angry and hurt by God. I felt like He no longer cared for me and I didn't matter. I forgot that He was my loving Heavenly Father. I felt so abandoned by Him."

Because Greta forgot her identity as Abba's child, within just a short time of her mom's passing, she found herself in a season of temptation, and she gave in. She told me, "Not long after the death of my mom my heart was so hard and I found myself in a situation I thought would never happen. I cheated on my husband. Although there was a part of me that felt horrible and guilty, there was also a part of me that didn't care."

Because she forgot who she was "in Christ," and forgot how much Abba loved her as His child, and forgot that He had a wonderful plan for her life, she gave into temptation.

She continues: "After 4 months of lying and cheating I finally couldn't stand being trapped. I felt like I was being choked to death with my very own hands. My husband came home from work one day and saw me sitting on the couch. I had been crying for hours. I finally told him the truth. I expected him to leave me. In fact, in a way I wanted to free him from me because he deserved much better. After knowing how God abandoned me, being abandoned by someone else wouldn't matter either."

Though her husband was hurt and stunned by the revelation he decided not to leave, but rather told her that they were going to work through it. A short time later they joined our New Life Family and God began to slowly restore their relationship. They did the hard work of Christian counseling—learning to forgive and be forgiven by each other, and by God. They opened up their lives to the healing grace of Jesus. And, most of all, Greta said she rediscovered that God was her Abba, that she was His little girl, and that He really did care for her deeply.

She said, "Looking back I can now see so clearly. I can see that what happened was—my mom died. That's all that happened. I made up the entire story that God didn't love or care for me, and had abandoned me and that I didn't matter to Him. Because of the story that I made up, my life was almost shattered. My actions affected everyone around me and nearly destroyed my marriage. What was real was that Father God did love me. I did matter to him, and He did care for me. He had never abandoned me."

Today, it is such a joy to see Greta and her husband in a beautiful relationship, and both of them serving in God's family together!

The truth is, our security in our identity as Abba's child helps us stand strong against temptation and not give in. And if we have given in, it's also what gives us the courage and boldness to seek forgiveness and restoration.

Jesus's identity, and personal security, as Abba's Child is what gave Him the strength to overcome temptation. The Bible says, *"Then Jesus (right after His baptism) was led by the Spirit into the desert to be tempted by the devil. After fasting forty days and forty nights, he was hungry. The tempter came to him and said, 'If you are the* **Son of God**, *tell these stones to become bread'"* (Matthew 4:1-3 NIV).

Three different times Satan asked Jesus the same thing, *"If you are the* **Son of God...**" All three of these temptations are intended to challenge the authority of the Jordan experience, where Jesus was baptized. Father God had just finished saying, *"You are my beloved Son in whom I am well pleased."* Now Satan, through these temptations, asked, *"Are you sure you are the Son of God? Maybe the desert heat got to Your head and You had some illusion that you heard a voice from heaven saying you are God's Son-Servant-Beloved."*

How did Jesus overcome His temptations? By referring back to His relationship with His Abba.

When we know that we are the Father's child-servant-beloved we have the strength to endure the same three temptations Christ endured.

First, when we're tempted to feed our appetites inappropriately, whether it's the abuse of wine, women (or men) or wealth, our Abba experience will keep us from giving in. We'll say, "Father knows what's best for me, and He says this is out of bounds, so I refuse to do that."

Then, when we're tempted to fight and claw for power, prestige, and position, our Abba experience will keep us from giving in. We'll say, "I trust my Father's heart and I know that promotion comes from the Lord. He will put me where He wants me."

Also, when we're tempted to worship the gods of our culture...the gods of greed, lust, and power...our Abba experience will cause us to say, "I will worship only the One who deserves it—the only One who can really satisfy my soul—God my Father, and Jesus my Big Brother."

The Bible says, "Therefore, it was necessary for [Jesus] to be in every respect like us, his brothers and sisters, so that he could be our merciful and faithful High Priest before God...Since he himself has gone through suffering and temptation, he is able to help us when we are being tempted" (Hebrews 2:17, 18 NLT). The good news is, Jesus knows the temptation you're going through, He feels your struggle, and He is also more than able to help you win the battle. Because the Son of God overcame temptation, you and I, God's sons and daughters, have power to overcome temptation.

Prayer is the key! Jesus was able to resist temptation because He was always renewing His relationship with His Abba through prayer. He knew this was the key to overcoming temptation, this is why, when He was in the Garden of Gethsemane with His followers, He asked them: "Why are you sleeping?" "Get up and pray that you will not fall into temptation" (Luke 22:46 TEV).

He was telling them this because, at that very moment, He was being tempted to not go to the cross. But through His talk with His Father He was able to say, "Ok, Abba, I submit to Your plans for my life."

Pray, develop your communication with God your Father, and you'll find yourself a whole lot stronger when temptation comes. That will protect your relationships from harm.

ENDURE WHEN YOU'RE CRITICIZED

There is another relational benefit to knowing your personal security "In Christ." It helps you to endure when you're criticized.

Criticism, or the fear of criticism, sabotages many people when they are at their most defining moments of life. Whether it's facing a decision to change their personal lives—their health, finances, or attitudes—or to go for a dream, or to confront an issue, or to start a business or ministry, sometimes we think, "What are people going to say?" "What if I fail?" "I know who I am, my weaknesses and tendencies, how can I do this?" Or others may say to us, "Who do you think you are? I know the real you, you can't do that." Or, they may launch into a tirade criticizing our imperfections, faults, and defects.

When this criticism happens, our personal insecurities are revealed. And this has messed up more marriages, careers, ministries, and dreams and goals than anything else I know.

For years, this really messed me up for two reasons. 1) I was always trying to make everyone happy; 2) I was always trying to be perfect. Have you discovered yet that trying to be perfect wears you out, and sets you up for chronic poor self-worth? Because none of us can be perfect.

And the problem with trying to make everyone happy is, when I made "Camp A" happy, "Camp B" started criticizing me; when I made "Camp B" happy, "Camp A" started criticizing me.

Why do we try to do what even God can't do? We do it because we don't like to be criticized; we like to make everyone happy.

These days I can still fall into that people-pleasing trap, but I don't struggle with it nearly as much as I used to. Why? Because years ago I started finding my identity in being Abba's child. I started living for an audience of One. And I started offering my true self, with all its humanity and imperfections, to Jesus Christ, and letting Him heal me.

The good news is, when we discover our true self, as Abba's child, we can endure the most severe criticism.

Jesus Christ was the most criticized Man to ever walk this planet, and because He knew He was Abba's Son-Servant-Beloved, Jesus was able to face it all.

He showed us how to face the most hurtful kind of criticism, criticism that comes from those closest to us—our family and friends. Jesus went back to His hometown of Nazareth and was met with criticism: *"Where did he get all his wisdom and the power to perform such miracles?...He's just the carpenter, the son of Mary...." They were deeply offended and refused to believe in him. Then Jesus told them, 'A prophet is honored everywhere* **except in his own hometown and among his relatives and his own family'"** (Mark 6:2, 3, 4 NLT).

Have you noticed that those we grow up with "in our hometown, and among our relatives and family," who should be cheering us on the most, can sometimes be the ones who criticize us the most?

Even Jesus' own brothers criticized Him because they didn't believe in Him. Even Jesus' closest friends criticized Him. At one point, when He raised the bar of following Him as totally devoted disciples, many of His closet friends and followers criticized Him and then forsook Him.

And even the religious leaders of the day, the Pharisees, the spiritual power-brokers, were Jesus' sharpest critics. There are times when those who are supposed to be spiritual leaders, representing the Father's heart, can be our harshest critics. The Bible says, "So the Jewish leaders began harassing Jesus for breaking the Sabbath rules. But Jesus replied, 'My Father is always working, and so am I.' So the Jewish leaders tried all the harder to find a way to kill him. For he not only broke the Sabbath, he called God his Father, thereby making himself equal with God" (John 5:16-18 NLT).

The primary reason these religious leaders ultimately put Jesus on the cross is Jesus' claim to God as His Father, His Abba. "How could He talk about Jehovah, God Almighty, so flippantly?"

How did Jesus respond? He said, Oh, you're upset that I call God Abba? Watch this—and He proceeded to call God, "Father," eleven more times in this exchange! (John 5:19-23).

What was the source of His personal security? His identity as Abba's child. He said to His critics… "Your approval or disapproval means nothing to me, because I know you don't have God's love within you" (John 5:41 NLT). In other words, "If God loves me, and if I love me, but you don't love me, guess who's got the problem? I am not seeking your approval, and I already have My Abba's."

The next time you're criticized, justly or unjustly, and your insecurities begin to rise up, in that defining moment whisper in your heart… "I am Abba's child-servant-beloved. Because of Jesus, Father God loves me no matter how well I do on this project, performance, or presentation. I'm going to give it my best shot, but no matter how it turns out, in Father's eyes, I'm still okay, loved, and safe."

GIVE YOU TRANSCENDENT PEACE

There is one more personal and relational benefit to you knowing your personal security as Abba's child, and that is it will give you transcendent peace to help you when you walk through the dark nights of the soul.

Every one of us knows what it is like to unexpectedly enter a season of intense difficulty, where it seems like we're experiencing the death of something in our lives that once had life—like the death of a dream, a relationship, a season of life, or a career. When this happens, so many times relationships blow apart. Why? Often it's because someone didn't have their identity and security in the right thing. Their identity was in that job, or relationship, or bank account.

What holds us together in our relationships, when we go through these dark nights of the soul, is our personal security that's wrapped up in our identity as Abba's child-servant-beloved. That is what gives us transcendent inner peace. That, in turn, brings peace into our relationships during tough times.

Jesus experienced this at three different times during the most difficult moments at the close of His life—at the Last Supper, the Garden of Gethsemane, and the Cross.

First, the Last Supper. Just hours before entering His dark night of the soul, when He would be arrested, tried, tortured and then crucified, Jesus reclined at the table at dinner and told His followers, *"...the time is coming...when you will be scattered, each one going his own way, leaving me alone. Yet I am not alone because the Father is with me"* (John 16:32 NLT).

Jesus knew what He was about to suffer. He knew He was going to need support more than ever before, and yet He also knew that His closest friends were all going to leave Him alone. What gave Jesus peace in spite of this? He knew Abba was with Him. *"All may forsake me, **but I am not alone because the Father is with me**."*

There are times in life when those closest to you—a spouse, friend, or loved one—might leave you alone. If they walk away or walk out, what's going to fill the vacuum of that lost love? Only one thing can—your relationship with Jesus Christ, and our heavenly Father. Only His love will sustain you, and let you know that you are not alone.

After dinner that night, we see the second time Jesus depended on His identity as Abba's child to bring inner peace. And that is in Garden of Gethsemane. He took His disciples to this Garden to pray. The Bible says, *"He went on a little farther and bowed with his face to the ground, praying, 'My Father! If it is possible, let this cup of suffering be taken away from me. Yet I want your will to be done, not mine'"* (Matthew 26:39 NLT). When we are in our own

Garden of Gethsemane, experiencing the death of a relationship, a dream, or a season of life our life, it is our relationship with Father God that holds us steady.

Some of you reading this are in your Garden where you've been begging God to let the cup of suffering pass from you. He may do that for you, but, like Christ, He may not. In either case, Abba tells you that He will not abandon you. It is here in our Garden that we most learn to yield to God's plans and purposes for our lives, even when it doesn't make sense. It is here that we learn to trust Abba's love for us.

Finally we come to the cross. The cross came after Jesus was falsely accused and criticized at a mock trial; after He was beaten with fists and His back whipped violently with the cat of nine tails; after a crown of thorns pressed into his brow and His beard was plucked. After all that the Roman soldiers took Jesus out to the Place of the Skull and pierced His hands and feet with spikes, as they nailed Him to the cross.

It was while Jesus was suffering in unimaginable agony on that cross that He again turned to His Abba and said, "Father, forgive them for they don't know what they're doing." That is what gives us the peace and power to do the same thing when we are on our cross, being innocently crucified by the spikes of false accusations, or by uncontrollable circumstances, or by intense attacks on our personal security. Because we know we are Abba's child we can say like our Big Brother Jesus said, "Father, forgive them."

Finally, when Jesus is about to take His very last breath He finds inner peace by looking to His Abba one last time. He lifts His eyes from the cross to the dark heavens above and shouts, *"Father, into your hands I entrust my spirit"* (Luke 23:46 GW). Then He breathed His last breath and died.

When we truly know we are Abba's child we can trust the Father even when we don't understand Him and His ways. We too can say, "Father, into Your hands I entrust my relationship that's falling apart, my child that's spinning out of control, or this friendship that's crashing. Into Your hands I entrust this, because I know you are my Father and I am your beloved child."

This one relationship with Abba is the key to all the others in your life. If you know that you are loved by Abba, and by His Christ, then you find the energy to love others—even your enemies. If you are experiencing the security that comes from your identity as Father's child-servant-beloved then you are confident to move forward in all your relationships.

So, my friend, embrace who you are right now—Abba's child. Let the Father's love fill you. He's crazy about you!

"*[Jesus] went on a little farther and bowed with his face to the ground, praying, 'My Father! If it is possible, let this cup of suffering be taken away from me. Yet I want your will to be done, not mine.'*"

Matthew 26:39 NLT

Chapter Ten

KEEPING LOVE THE MAIN THING

"Love doesn't make the world go 'round. Love is what makes the ride worthwhile" (Franklin P. Jones). Throughout our journey together in this book, I've repeatedly emphasized that love is the main thing in all of our relationships. And the main thing is to keep the main thing, "the main thing!"

Jesus was the one who said that all of the Law boils down to this: Loving God and loving people. All that matters is love! That's what Paul the Apostle said as well: *"If you are a follower of Christ Jesus...All that matters is your faith that makes you love others"* (Galatians 5:6 CEV). In all of our relationships the main thing is love!

Now, if love is the main thing then we really need to define what love is, because there are so many opinions out there about what love is. For example, recently, someone asked a bunch of kids the question, "What is love"? Here are a few of their answers:

- "Love is that first feeling you feel before all the bad stuff gets in the way."

- "Love is when a girl puts on perfume and a boy puts on shaving cologne and they go out and smell each other."

- "When my grandmother got arthritis, she couldn't bend over and paint her toenails anymore. So my grandfather does it for her all the time, even when his hands got arthritis too. That's love."

- "Love is when my mommy makes coffee for my daddy and she takes a sip before giving it to him, to make sure the taste is OK."

- "Love is when you tell a guy you like his shirt, then he wears it every day."

- "My mommy loves me more than anybody. You don't see anyone else kissing me to sleep at night."

- "Love is when mommy gives daddy the best piece of chicken."

In the love chapter of the Bible, First Corinthians 13, Paul gives us both the importance of love and the true definition of love. First let's look at the importance of love in our relationships.

LOVING OTHERS IS MORE IMPORTANT THAN MY WORDS

Paul says, *"If I could speak all the languages of earth and of angels, but didn't love others, I would only be a noisy gong or a clanging cymbal"* (1 Corinthians 13:1 NLT). The writer of this love chapter was speaking to Christ-followers who had the special ability to speak to God in a prayer language—a spiritual language they hadn't learned naturally. It was a language given to them by the Holy Spirit.

And, man, were they proud of being able to speak in a spiritual language! But Paul says, Listen, you can speak in a heavenly language all you want to—and you should want to—but if you're not motivated by love it doesn't matter at all.

My church tradition growing up was Pentecostal. And in those Pentecostal churches there were some very fine God-loving people. But in my experience, sometimes those who spoke in tongues the loudest were also the meanest! Now I'm not minimizing praying in a spiritual language, because that is truly one of the gifts that God gives to His children. But God says, "It doesn't matter if you are fluent in a heavenly language or if you're fluent in ten earthly languages, if you don't have love then your beautiful language means nothing!"

LOVING OTHERS IS MORE IMPORTANT THAN MY KNOWLEDGE

Paul says, "I may have the gift of prophecy. I may understand all the secret things of God and have all knowledge...But...if I do not have love, then I am nothing" (1 Corinthians 13:2 NCV). You and I may be the most knowledgeable people on the planet, but if we don't have love in our lives then all that we know is worthless.

The truth is, our knowledge alone will never solve the world's problems. Look at how knowledge has increased since 1900. According to Buckminster Fuller, who created the "Knowledge Doubling Curve," human knowledge doubled approximately every century until 1900. By the end of World War II, knowledge was doubling every 25 years. Today, on average, human knowledge is doubling every 13 months. According to IBM, the build out of the "internet of things" will lead to the doubling of knowledge every 12 hours.

But in spite of all this new knowledge we still have war, terrorism, crime, abuse, prejudice, hatred and violence. Why? Because what the world needs is not more knowledge, it needs more love.

Can you imagine what would happen if every single person on planet earth suddenly started to love one another unconditionally, to accept one another completely, and forgive one another totally? What would our world be like? That would be utopia—heaven on earth.

Until Jesus returns to earth that kind of utopia is not going to happen, but we can begin practicing that kind of love in our family, workplace, schools, and neighborhoods. We may not be able to experience heaven on earth right now, but we can bring a little bit of heaven to earth by loving one another.

LOVING OTHERS IS MORE IMPORTANT THAN MY BELIEFS

All my life I have seen people who think that if they believe certain truths about God and the Bible, that makes them a true Christ-follower. But nothing can be further from the truth. Following Christ is much more than believing doctrinal truths. Being a Christ-follower is a life of love.

"Even if I had the gift of faith so that I could speak to a mountain and make it move, I would still be worth nothing at all without love" (1 Corinthians 13:2 TLB).

When I was a kid growing up in my daddy's church, there was an elderly man there who was the patriarch of the church. There was no doubt that he was "the man." Everyone looked to him because he had founded the church and was Mr. Bible-answer Man. He knew everything doctrinally!

In my mind I can still see him sitting in the pew on the front row in "his" spot. He always had his arms folded when daddy preached. And if "the man" said Amen to something dad said the rest of the congregation would say Amen too. But if he dropped his head and wagged it, to show some kind of disapproval at what dad said, everyone else would do the same.

At first, he was very impressive to a little kid like me—all that grey hair, large physique, booming voice, and authority. Impressive! But over the next two years I saw the real Mr. Bible-answer Man, as he revealed his heart full of "isms": legalism, racism, egotism, narcissism, and mean-ism. It all came to a head one day when, in a fit of anger, he punched my dad right in front of us kids. Shortly thereafter he led a coup to get my dad ousted from his pastorate. He had his beliefs, his doctrines, and his theology—but he had no love.

Later, as I studied church history as an adult, I discovered that the man in my dad's church wasn't an exception to the rule. I discovered that over the last two millennium there have been many experts in theology and doctrine who, in the Name of Christ, did some horribly unloving things. The Crusades, the Inquisition, the witch-hunts in Salem, the KKK during the Civil Rights Movement, etc...

Faith and belief must all be wrapped in God's love if they are to have any value. Yes, let's "get" our beliefs, but let's make sure we "get" God's love! Love is always our motivator!

LOVING OTHERS IS MORE IMPORTANT THAN MY GENEROSITY

First Corinthians 13:3 says, "If I gave everything I have to the poor and even sacrificed my body...but didn't love others, I would have gained nothing" (NLT). I would be of no value whatsoever.

Can we give without loving? Sure. Some people give just to get back. Some people give trying to ease a guilty conscious for some wrong in their past. Some people give in order to control other people. And then there are those who give for prestige. They give in order to get others to notice that they are a great giver. None of that is giving with love.

Love is giving like God gives. It's when in our relationships we give to others freely, generously, and graciously, from a heart of love.

LOVING OTHERS IS MORE IMPORTANT THAN MY SUCCESS

Paul says, "So, no matter what I say, what I believe, and what I do, I'm bankrupt without love" (1 Corinthians 13:3 MSG).

We can have the biggest home in town, or the biggest bank account, or the biggest business or church, but if we have all of that but we don't have love, we aren't truly successful. Love is the main thing.

A person who never experienced that in her lifetime was one of the biggest sex symbols of modern times, Marilyn Monroe. Marilyn had unbelievable success as an actress and model; her films grossed over 200 million dollars. She had fame and money, but she didn't have what she craved most—love.

She never knew her real father, and when she was a child, her mother was mentally unstable, so she was moved from foster home to foster home. And in some of those homes she was sexually exploited.

As a little girl she craved love, but didn't find it. And then at age 16 she married, hoping to find the illusive love. But she didn't find it there either. She went on to wed other men as well, but didn't discover love there either.

Finally, at 36 years old, at the top of her career, Marilyn Monroe took a bottle of sleeping pills and ended her life. As the country song says, she was "looking for love in all the wrong places." What a sad and tragic end to a beautiful soul.

RELATIONSHIPS ARE MORE IMPORTANT THAN ACCOMPLISHMENTS!

Paul tells us that love is more important than anything else in life! It is the main thing. So, because that is true, it's vital that we know what love really is. How are we to love others? Well, let me give you one more kid's viewpoint of love to show you what real love is: "Love is when you tell someone something bad about yourself and you're scared they won't love you anymore. But then you get surprised because not only do they still love you, they love you even more."

Real love is **UNCONDITIONAL LOVE.** It's the kind of love that we all crave in the deepest part of our being. And it's the kind of love that God has for us. It's also the kind of love that God wants us to have for others.

The Apostle John said, *"Dear friends, if this is how God loved us, then we should love one another"* (1 John 4:11 GNT). Jesus said, *"My command is this: Love each other as I have loved you"* (John 15:12 NIV). With God's example, we know how to love each other. God loves us unconditionally and so we are to love each other unconditionally.

So, what does unconditional love look like in your everyday life? Paul tells us in First Corinthians 13.

TO LOVE UNCONDITIONALLY MEANS I LOVE OTHERS WITHOUT GIVING UP ON THEM

Paul says, *"Love never gives up; and its faith, hope and patience never fail"* (1 Corinthians 13:7 GNT). Unconditional love never says, "Well, I like her, but I don't love her anymore." Or, "We've lost that loving feeling." Love that's based solely on emotion is kind of like teen-age love—teen-age love is a feeling you feel when you feel that what you feel is a feeling you never felt before!

The truth is, feelings of love are wonderful, but they come and go. What keeps you together in your relationships is unconditional love.

Unconditional love says, "I choose to love you whether you've got make-up on or not. I choose to love you whether you put the seat up on the potty or not. I choose to love you whether you text me right back or not. I choose to love you whether you've picked up your dirty socks or not."

If our relationships are based on feelings rather than choice then we're in for fickle relationships, because emotions are totally erratic and irregular.

Consider the young bride talking to her friend. She said, "I simply can't stand my husband's nasty disposition. Before we got married he was so nice and now he's so irritable. Why, he's made me so jittery that I'm losing weight." Her friend asks her, "Well, why don't you leave the sorry sucker?" She said, "Oh, I'm going to. I'm just waiting until he gets me down to 120 pounds!"

Love is not a feeling. It creates feelings, but it is not feelings. Many times we have to choose to love someone. I know that it's hard for some folks to believe, but there have been times in my many years with Lydia, the love of my life, that I have had to choose to love her. Yes, I've felt deep emotions of love and adoration for my wife. But I've also felt other emotions for my wife as well—if you know what I mean. And I think there's been a time or two that she's experienced some feelings for me that weren't exactly "a quiver in her liver."

It has been in those tough times, when we didn't feel "in love" that we've had to "love by faith." It's when we've lost that loving feeling, that we've chosen to love each other. And because we didn't give up on each other, eventually, we found that loving feeling again.

The truth is, love is something you can choose to do! You can choose to love your friends, your kids, your spouse, and your neighbors. That's what unconditional love is. Love never gives up, it's always persistent.

God gave us a wonderful, yet hard to believe, story of this kind of love in the Bible. It's the story about a pastor whose wife was a prostitute. That man's name was Hosea. His wife left him and was out prostituting herself out on the streets. I'm sure the gossip in the church was intense! I'm sure folks were telling the pastor to divorce her. But, amazingly, God tells Pastor Hosea to do the absurd. God says, *"Go, show your love to your wife again, though she is loved by another and is an adulteress. Love her as the Lord loves the Israelites, though they turn to other gods..."* (Hosea 3:1 NIV). Hosea did what God said and took his wife back and loved her unconditionally in spite of what she'd done.

That's unconditional love. The kind of love that persists, endures, and doesn't give up, no matter what. That's the kind of love God has for us and the kind He wants us to have toward one another.

TO LOVE UNCONDITIONALLY MEANS
I LOVE OTHERS WITH NO LIMITS

In other words, I accept our differences, I tolerate your idiosyncrasies, and I'm patient with your wonderfully weird ways!

I've heard a lot of people say to others, "When you change and become more like me then I'll love you and accept you." That's not unconditional love, is it? Unconditional love is saying, "I love you in spite of yourself. And I know you love me in spite of myself!"

Paul says, "*Love is patient and kind; it is not jealous or conceited or proud; love is not ill-mannered*" (1 Corinthians 13:4-5 GNT). That means we accept one another's differences. We love with no limits.

Now, when I say we "accept" our differences, I am not saying we approve of all our differences. Because, as I said earlier, you can accept somebody without approving everything about them.

The Bible says, "*Accept one another, then, just as Christ accepted you...*" (Romans 15:7 NIV). How has Christ accepted you? Just as you are! That's unconditional acceptance, and unconditional love, and it has the power to unite people who are very different from each other.

This kind of accepting, unconditional love is one of the reasons why I believe God has blessed the community of faith that I get to lead. If you were to show up on an average Sunday you would see people gathered at New Life Center from every background imaginable. We are a picture of what heaven is going to be like—red, yellow, black and white, old and young, rich and poor. Just beautiful!

For going on three decades our heartbeat in our New Life Family has been, "We will accept anybody here!" We throw out a broad welcome mat! And we do get criticism for it. In fact, one critic called us Low Life Center, instead of New Life Center—"Because they just let anybody go there!" We wear that label as a badge of honor! Everybody is welcomed, no matter how different they are!

We tell people all the time, "Here at New Life, we don't care if you are black, white, brown, red, yellow, pink or blue—you are accepted! We don't care if you are Pentecostal, Catholic, Baptist or Buddhist—you are accepted! We don't care if you are the poorest person or the richest person in Kern County—you are accepted! We don't care if you are a Democrat or a Republican or an Independent or a nothing—you are accepted!"

I am convinced that our heart of unconditional love, acceptance and forgiveness—our embrace of diversity—is what has allowed us to do what most church growth experts told us could not be done... have a multi-ethnic, multi-generational, and multi-denominational church family.

What would happen in our homes if we had this kind of revival of unconditional love? For years Lydia and I experienced conflict in our relationship because we were always expecting each other to think, feel, and act like the each other. It was only when I began to accept her uniqueness and love her unconditionally, and she began to accept my weirdness and love me unconditionally, that we began to experience real intimacy.

Aren't you glad that God doesn't put conditions on us before He loves us? Can you imagine God saying to you, "I'll love you when you get your act together, when you no longer make mistakes, when you measure up to my standard"? No! God says, "I love you in spite of your flops, failures, and foibles. I love you with no strings attached, no conditions to be met other than you trusting in me." That's how God wants us to love one another—to love completely.

TO LOVE UNCONDITIONALLY MEANS I LOVE OTHERS BY SEEKING TO MEET THEIR NEEDS

Paul says, "[Love] is not rude, it is **not self-seeking**, it is not easily angered, it keeps no record of wrongs" (1 Corinthians 13:5 NIV).

Does that kind of love sound a little different than what our world practices? The motto of a lot of people is, "I've got to do what's best for me" or "I've got to look out for number one." With our culture's self-centered ways it's easy for any of us to get caught up in this egocentric mind-set. By the way, do you know how you know if you've become an egomaniac? One man said, "An egotist is a person who is me-deep in conversation." But there is one good thing about an egotist—at least he doesn't talk about other people!

If I'm going to love unconditionally like God loves, then I have to seek to meet others' needs, not just my own.

Recently I was told about a couple who was getting a divorce. When I asked why they were splitting up I was told that the man had said, "It's because she doesn't meet my sexual needs." I asked, "You mean they don't have a normal intimate relationship with each other?" This person told me, "Oh no, they have sex but she just doesn't please him." I have to be honest with you, when I heard that I wanted to go slap him—in Jesus' Name, of course. I thought, you selfish, little clod. You don't need a divorce, you need a whipping! Then you need to repent of your selfishness and go back and apologize to your wife and begin seeking to meet her needs.

This principle applies to all areas of our relationships. We must love unconditionally by seeking to meet the needs of others. And what will ultimately happen when we are not self-seeking? Many times our needs will be met as well. The Bible says, "...he who refreshes others will himself be refreshed" (Proverbs 11:25 NIV). Jesus said, "Give and it will be given to you" (Luke 6:38 NIV).

Love is more than just a feeling, it's something we do, it's an action. The Bible says, "But if someone who is supposed to be a Christian has money enough to live well, and sees a brother in need, and won't help him—how can God's love be within him? Little children, let us stop just saying we love people; let us really love them, **and show it by our actions**" (1 John 3:17-18 TLB).

God says, "Don't just say it, show it! Show it by trying to meet others' needs. That's true love.

TO LOVE UNCONDITIONALLY MEANS I LOVE OTHERS ETERNALLY

In other words, unconditional love is our commitment to love others for a lifetime; it is lasting, and is going to be consistent over the long haul.

Paul says, "Love is eternal" (1 Corinthians 13:8 GNT). God's kind of love is eternal and everlasting; it is a forever kind of love. It can always be counted on, and is ever true.

When I was a child growing up in church I always saw God as a vengeful God, who was just waiting for me to blow it so He could whack me. I saw His love as capricious, moody, and conditioned by how well I was keeping the moral code that particular day. As a result, I felt I had to get re-saved every Sunday. I'd get born again, again and again! There were a lot of days in my teenage years that I woke up thinking, "I wonder if God's going to love me today?"

But then in my early 20's I experienced God's grace, revealed through the cross of Christ, for the first time in my life. I discovered a God who told me, "James, wherever you go, whatever you do, *my* love is going to be there for you. *My* love is not fickle or temperamental. And it is not based on your goodness, but on *my* goodness."

I was ambushed by God's unconditional love, and it began to radically transform my life. Over time, the ongoing experience of God's unconditional love instilled a sense of security in my soul that has carried me through a lot of dark days.

When you and I experience the forever kind of love that God offers us, we're able to offer that same kind of love to others. The kind of love that says, "You can count on my love. No matter what you do or where you go I'm going to love you."

You say, "But, James, what about my child that's gone off the deep end of drug or alcohol addiction, or steeped in sexual sins, and they're in rebellion? I've had to set boundaries and make them leave my home." That's called "tough love," and Father God does the same with us. Sometimes, though it may not feel like it, tough love is the most loving thing you can do.

But if you've planted seeds of unconditional love in their lives, the day will come when they will bottom out and remember that love, acceptance, and forgiveness is waiting for them.

Remember the story of the prodigal son? The father had to watch his son walk away from the safety and security of his home, walk away from all the truths he was taught growing up, and walk away from his God. But did the father run after him? No, he entrusted him to God and allowed him to go learn the hard lessons that life teaches all of us.

Now, he could have been a good co-dependent and said, "I love you too much to let you hurt. Let me rescue you and fix you—just one more time."

But he didn't. He loved his son enough to let go of the controls and let God and life teach the tough lessons. And when the son finally bottomed out and came home broken, ashamed, and humbled, had the love of the father changed? Absolutely not!

In one of the most moving scenes in the entire Bible the son comes home covered with dried up pig slop and dirt (not kosher for a Jewish boy). And when the father saw him coming he was filled with compassion and ran out to meet him. He threw his arms around his wayward son and kissed him repeatedly—as if to say, "Son, I loved you then, when you were clean and together, and I love you now, when you are dirty and broken."

That's unconditional love! That's the healing kind of love! That's God's forever kind of love! Parents, the greatest gift you can give your children is unconditional love; husbands and wives, the greatest gift you can give your mate is unconditional love; friends, the greatest gift you can give another friend, is unconditional love.

And how do we give that unconditional love? By first experiencing it ourselves. We can only give what we have received. Today, remember how much God loves you unconditionally by remembering the cross. See Jesus hanging there in your place, saying to you, "I love you this much! I love you so much it hurts!"

As I close this chapter and come to the conclusion of this book, I want to pray a prayer of blessing over you now, that you will experience God's unconditional love. It's Paul's prayer for his friends, and it is my prayer for you, my friend:

"And I ask [God] that with both feet planted firmly on love, you'll be able to take in with all [followers of Jesus] the extravagant dimensions of Christ's love. Reach out and experience the breadth! Test its length! Plumb the depths! Rise to the heights! Live full lives, full in the fullness of God."

Ephesians 3:17-19 MSG

EPILOGUE

So let me ask you as we come to the end of our journey together—"How is your most important relationship, your relationship with Father God?" Some of you are in a good place. That is awesome! But some of you are in a place that is far from Father. Like the Prodigal Son you've drifted away from Abba's home, looking for love in all the wrong places, and you feel totally like you're in a faraway land. Hear Father God say to you, "...*with deep love I will take you back*" (Isaiah 54:7 GNT). Simply come back home to Him right now.

Some of you have never had a true relationship with God through Jesus Christ. I invite you to say yes to God's offer of forgiveness for your past sins, power to change your life, and the promise of everlasting life in Heaven someday. If you do step over the faith line, you too will have a new identity as Father God's child-servant-beloved, and you will find new energy to love others the same way you've been loved.

If that is you, I ask you to pray this in your heart: "Father God, I believe You are a God of love. And You loved me so much that You sent Your son Jesus to die for my sins so I could be forgiven. I'm sorry for my sins and I want to live the rest of my life the way You want me to. Please put Your Spirit in my life to direct me. And as You have loved me, I want to love others in my life the same way. In Jesus' Name. Amen."